South-East England and East Anglia

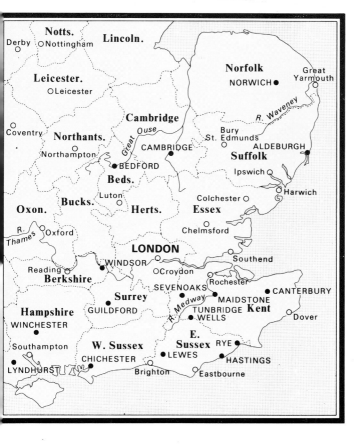

Regional Guides to Britain

South-East England and East Anglia

Roger Higham
Series Editor **Kenneth Lowther**

Ward Lock Limited · London

Dedication

To my late, dear wife, Isabel

© Ward Lock Limited 1983

First published in Great Britain in 1983
by Ward Lock Limited, 82 Gower Street,
London WC1E 6EQ, a Pentos Company.

Designed by Peter Holroyd
Maps prepared by Oxford Cartographers Limited

Text filmset in Century Schoolbook
by MS Filmsetting Limited, Frome, Somerset

Printed in Great Britain by
Blantyre Printing & Binding Co. Limited,
Blantyre, Scotland

British Library Cataloguing in Publication Data
Higham, Roger
   South-East England—(Regional guides to Britain)
   1. England—Description and travel—Guide-books
   I. Title   II. Series
   914.22′04858   DA650

   ISBN 0-7063-6226-8

The black and white illustrations were kindly supplied by
the following:
p. 31, 40, 59, D. Warren; p. 139, 153, A. C. Allen;
All other photographs by British Tourist Authority.

Front Cover: Goudhurst, Kent (British Tourist Authority)
Frontispiece: Beachy Head and lighthouse

Contents

Chichester 76

Chichester – Fishbourne – Bosham – Portsmouth –
Portchester – Uppark – Singleton – Amberley – Arundel –
Chichester

Winchester 85

Winchester – Romsey – Mottisfont – King's Somborne –
Stockbridge – Micheldever – Alresford – Chawton – Selborne –
Winchester

Lyndhurst 95

Lyndhurst – Rufus Stone – Fritham – Moyles Court – Burley –
Brockenhurst – Lymington – Beaulieu – Lyndhurst

Guildford 103

Guildford – Godalming – Hindhead – Haslemere – Midhurst –
Petworth – Chiddingfold – Dunsfold – Leith Hill – Dorking –
Polesden Lacey – Guildford

Windsor 112

Windsor – Runnymede – Ascot – Wokingham – Sonning –
Chiltern Hills – West Wycombe – High Wycombe –
Hughenden Manor – Cliveden – Bray – Windsor

Bedford 122

Bedford – Elstow – Houghton House – Woburn Abbey –
Ampthill – Sandy – St Neots – Godmanchester – St Ives –
Huntingdon – Kimbolton – Bedford

Cambridge 130

Cambridge – Grantchester – Wimpole Hall – Saffron Walden –
Thaxted – Castle Hedingham – Sudbury – Lavenham –
Bury St Edmunds – Cambridge

Aldeburgh 140

Aldeburgh – Snape – Orford – Woodbridge – Colchester –
East Bergholt – Flatford – Framlingham – Aldeburgh

Norwich 148

Index 159

Canterbury

Tourist Information Office
Longmarket, tel 66567

Population 33,150

Theatres
Gulbenkian, University of Kent, Giles Lane
Marlowe, under construction in old Odeon cinema, The Friars

Cinema
ABC, St George's Place

Museums
Royal Museum, High Street
Westgate Museum (arms and armour)
Buffs Regimental Museum, High Street

Places of Interest

Westgate	Castle
Eastbridge Hospital	City Walls
Greyfriars	Roman pavement, Butchery Lane
Poor Priests' Hospital	Christ Church Cathedral
St Mildred's Church	St Augustine's Abbey

A tour of South-East England could not begin at a more suitable place than Canterbury, a city that blends fascinatingly ancient, medieval, and modern buildings and traditions.

A settlement existed here in pre-Roman times; as *Durovernum Cantiacorum* it was the hub of radial roads from the ports to London, with a typical Roman grid of streets containing baths, town-houses, a theatre, and defensive walls. The incoming Germanic mercenaries of the fifth century ruined the Roman city, but later it became King Ethelbert of Kent's capital and St Augustine's primatial see, with two great abbeys. The accident of Archbishop Becket's murder in 1170 brought it pilgrims from all England and attendant prosperity, declining only with the sixteenth-century Reformation.

A quick tour might begin at Westgate, the only survivor of the new gates built in the 1380s, with new walls. From the gate, St Peter's Street bisects the city; the houses on either side are sometimes older than their brick façades might indicate. One branch of the River Stour passes before the Westgate, another beneath the road at Eastbridge, where a gabled cloth-hall called the Weavers faces a medieval hospital founded by Archbishop Becket. Beyond the Post Office turn right into Stour Street, and right again under an archway to see a' little stone building over the river called Greyfriars, given to the first group of Franciscan friars to settle in the city. Farther up Stour Street is the ancient Poor Priests' Hospital, and at the end of it is the basically Saxon St Mildred's Church. Nearby are the remains of Canterbury Castle, a huge Norman keep sadly dismantled for building stone in the eighteenth century. Turn left across the end of Castle Street, skirting the roundabout, and enter Dane John Gardens, behind a long stretch of the fourteenth-century city walls. Dane John, an artificial mound 'landscaped' in the eighteenth century, is probably a pre-Roman burial mound. Beyond the gardens is Roman Watling Street, passing through the Riding Gate, now bridged to carry the wall-walk. Past the Bus Station to your right, you arrive in the eastern end of the bisecting main street, here called St George's Street. Turn left along the arcades of modern shops and banks and right into Mercery Lane, between Boots and an ancient building rep-utedly once a pilgrims' hostel: its far end, in the Buttermarket, faces Christ Church Gate. Through it, you are confronted by the south-west porch of arguably the greatest cathedral church in England.

Enter by this porch, gaze up at the high forest-like nave roof, marvel at the steps to the screen, at the immense height of the tower ceiling. Go to the Martyrdom, where a tablet records the murder of St Thomas Becket, and mount the steps worn by pilgrims' feet to the place at which his shrine used to stand, and near which the Black Prince's still does. Look up at the glories of the Choir, and at the very early stained-glass windows all around the Corona, showing St Thomas's miracles. See these and many other wonders before leaving by the door from the Martyrdom, into the Cloisters to see the ancient monastery buildings, part ruins and part the basis of the King's School.

There is so much more to see in Canterbury, but this brief tour may serve perhaps to whet the appetite.

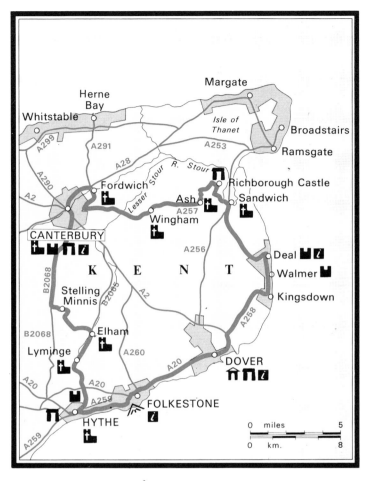

key

🏰 Church

🏠 House or Gardens

🏰 Castle

🏛 Archaeological Site

⩗ Viewpoint

𝑖 Tourist Information Centre

AA AA Service Centre

RAC RAC Service Centre

▮ Lighthouse

Canterbury – Stelling Minnis – Elham – Lyminge – Saltwood – Hythe – Sandgate – Folkestone – Dover – Walmer – Deal – Sandwich – Richborough – Wingham – Fordwich – Canterbury

Tour length 70 miles

Coastal defence is the dominant theme of this tour, as might be expected in an area of shore-line only twenty-odd miles away from a frequently hostile continental mainland. The country is hilly, green and fertile, the scenery sometimes spectacular, the villages entrancing, the variety astonishing. But the theme of defence recurs throughout, with no less than nine military fortifications of differing epochs, and six towns members of the Confederation of Cinque Ports, the medieval organisation responsible for furnishing the king with fighting ships. Every garden needs a fence, and Kent, the Garden of England, possessed of some of the most highly-rated agricultural land in the kingdom, needs a stronger one than most: it is also England's front line of defence.

Watling Street in Canterbury continues beyond the city wall as the Old Dover Road, the Roman link with the vital south-eastern port. A turning round the corner of St Lawrence cricket ground, the B2068, is the beginning of another Roman highway to another Roman port: Stone Street, going to Lympne. Its nearly undeviating directness, through lovely green farmland, tells the tale: Roman engineers, like their modern counterparts, believed in the shortest distance between two points. For variety, however, after 6½ miles of it take the turning left to Stelling Minnis. A minnis is a common, and this village, like an inhabited golf course, is spread out in all directions. Keeping right on this lane, past an old windmill, bear right again at the end of the village, through a hamlet engagingly named Wheelbarrow Town, then left into the dark mass of Lyminge Forest.

Stelling Minnis

Mainly of pine, this forest stretches all along the side of the valley into which you now descend; through it runs an intermittent stream called the Nailbourne. The B2065 road, into which you turn right, runs along the valley bottom into Elham.

Elham

On either side of Elham's widening street are sixteenth and seventeenth-century houses, of brick or timber. Opposite a timbered restaurant called *The Abbot's Fireside* turn sharp left into the little square: it is flanked on three sides by old brick houses, cottages, and an inn, and on the fourth by the church.

Lyminge

A little farther down the valley road, Lyminge lacks the same magic, but its church is interesting because it incorporates some of the tiles of a Roman villa on the site, and those who built it were some of the earliest English Christians.

The road now winds its way into the chalk hills, the North Downs, up and over them, emerging on the seaward side to dip sharply down to Hythe. On the steep decline stop awhile at a gateway to the right and see at a short distance the great medieval castle of Saltwood, where Becket's murderers gathered and paused on their way to Canterbury, in December 1170.

Hythe

A one-way system permits a round tour of Hythe, the lower road passing by a stretch of the Royal Military Canal, which is a defence-work built when a French invasion under Napoleon I was a possibility. It runs approximately along the course of the now-vanished River Limen, which gave Lyminge and Lympne their names, the Romans a naval base, *Portus Lemanis*, guarded by a fort now in total ruin, and the town of Hythe its reason for existence. By the early Middle Ages the river had silted up but its estuary was Hythe's harbour. When you turn at the western end of the town and return along its High Street, you pass between houses which once would have stood on the water's edge. Inns and taverns and shops line it, and under the pillared Town Hall a footpath leads steeply up to St Leonard's Church, whose crypt is full of bones of people dug up, it is thought, to make way for victims of the Black Death in 1350.

When the river silted up completely and the harbour disappeared, Hythe declined. Until then it had been one of the original south-eastern ports given rights and privileges by successive kings in return for providing fighting ships when needed. In Norman times (after 1066) these five ports became the Confederation of Cinque Ports: Hythe, Hastings, Romney, Dover, and Sandwich, with two others, Rye and Winchelsea, subsequently added and several more attached when financial duties weighed ever more heavily.

Hythe's road system is part of the A259, a south-coast road with its origins in Chichester; it now runs eastward along the base of high chalk cliffs **Sandgate** close by the sea. Sandgate lies at the foot of these cliffs, with some elegant Georgian terraces complete with typical wrought-iron balconies, and a surprising quantity of antique shops. A fragment remains of a coastal defence castle built by King Henry VIII in the 1540s.

The road climbs acutely to the cliff-top, and we **Folkestone** are in Folkestone, one of the most distinguished seaside holiday resorts of the south-east. The heights above the sea abound in hotels, some of spectacularly exotic Victorian extravagance. There is a pleasant promenade along the cliff-top, a concert-hall, and plenty of fine shops and stores in the town. Around the harbour is old fishing Folkestone, what is left of it.

The A20 road now takes you on to Dover, and there are places along it where, framed in a gap in the quiet green hills, you can catch a dramatic glimpse of the massive grey walls and turrets of Dover Castle.

Dover Dover, the 'Key to the Kingdom', is the nearest part of it to France, and therefore both the most valuable and the most vulnerable. Already, as you approached by the A20 from Folkestone you may have noticed on the hilltop to the right the square outline of a fort. This was the later type, built in 1859, the last occasion when trouble from France was feared. Down in the town, off the first roundabout past the railway station, signs direct you to the Painted House.

When the roundabout just referred to, and its adjacent road system, were being built in 1970, houses were demolished and clues were found: a descent of archaeologists on the spot established that here was the long-lost Roman fort of Dover. The Romans used Boulogne as their principal

Channel port, and Dover and Richborough as the main entry-points to their province of Britannia. Dover was the nearer and more convenient, lighthouses could be built on its two cliffs, and a fleet could be kept in its harbour (and at Lympne along the coast). The Painted House, large parts of which have been excavated and protected under permanent cover, was the fleet commandant's residence, outside a naval barracks. Eventually, attacks from Saxon pirates and a decline in the fleet's efficiency brought the army, in 270. The soldiers demolished the barracks and built a huge fort, a wall and bastion of which cut through part of the house and buried the rest, inadvertently preserving the mural painted plaster.

Dover is clearly still dominated by its harbour, now feverishly active with cross-channel traffic, and its medieval castle, accessible by the steep Castle Hill Road. In fact the site has been used by all ages: Iron-Age Britons built a hill-fort, the Romans built one of their lighthouses (which still stands, the tallest Roman building in England), and the Anglo-Saxons made a walled town against marauding Vikings. The little church of this town, much restored, survives alongside the lighthouse. William the Conqueror threw up a wooden stronghold, but it was Henry II, in the 1180s, who spent a fortune on the great square keep and curtain walls that still stand as solidly as when they were built. Subsequent alterations and additions were made by subsequent monarchs (it remained ever a royal castle for the defence of the realm), down to anti-aircraft platforms during the Second World War. There are medieval underground works, arms and armour in the keep, a shop and restaurant.

If it is lunch-time before you have even begun to climb Castle Hill, there are various kinds of hostelries in the town, at the foot of the hill and in the High Street, where the old Town Hall, called Maison Dieu, offers portraits and records of all Lord Wardens of the Cinque Ports.

Emerging at last from the castle and turning right, follow the last of Castle Hill to a roundabout from which you can take the A258 road, high and windy once more on the cliff-tops, going eastward, and for fun you might branch off right at Ringwould on the B2057 for a dive steeply down through the pretty cliff-hanging village of **Kingsdown** Kingsdown. The road then runs behind a high **Walmer** sand-dune and emerges at Walmer, where on your left you can see and visit on any day except Mondays one of Henry VIII's coastal castles, built when yet another French invasion was expected. It is in good repair because it was turned into the official residence of the Lord Warden of the Cinque Ports.

Deal About $1\frac{1}{4}$ miles away on the same road at Deal there is another castle of the same type and period. The Lifeboat Station on the sea-front to your right, with rows of fishing boats and yachts drawn up on the beach, and the long grey mass of the Royal Marine barracks on your left, precede the castle, which is the best of the kind in Kent and has been carefully kept by the Department of the Environment with a well-presented museum. These castles were built on a circular plan like a clover-leaf, with thick walls, gun-ports with a clear field of fire, and no tall towers offering easy targets for naval gunners at sea.

Deal's beach is a mile farther out to sea than it was when Julius Caesar beached his ships on it, as a result of sundry alterations in the channel current which blocked up Hythe's harbour and made the treacherous Goodwin Sands out of the former island of Lomea. Near the pier at Deal there is a detailed plan of these sands, showing the numerous wrecks on them. Deal is a fishing-town, with many little sea-food restaurants and inns along the front.

The A258 road leads you out of Deal and the landscape changes. Flat fields, dykes, marshes, and plenty of wind and sky accompany the way to Sandwich, for this is the estuary of the River Stour, which has suffered the same changes as the rest of this mutated sea-coast. Huge areas of land were once mud-flats at low tide, then bright shining water. The Isle of Thanet, the extreme south-eastern tip of England, has lost its nature, for once clear navigable water separated it from mainland Kent.

Sandwich Sandwich, on the Stour, is an ancient town, and an original Cinque Port, and since its streets are of maze-like complexity it is best to explore on foot. When approaching from Deal it is essential to branch right immediately after crossing the railway line and make for the car park on the Quay. Here can be seen the modest modern remnant of the once-great sea-port. Here too are the Fishergate and the Barbican, survivors from fourteenth-century fortifications. The parish church of St Clement's is nearby, with a Norman tower and Roman tiles in the walls. All about are the labyrinthine streets filled with houses of all ages and great charm. The Town Hall is a rebuilt replica, but contains inside much material from its original and a museum of Cinque Ports souvenirs.

Abandoning these charms and the lure of the celebrated golf courses, out on the dunes of the filled-in estuary, taking the A257 Canterbury road you must turn right before the railway crossing to follow a narrow and wriggling lane to **Richborough** Richborough Castle. Looking ahead you can see a promontory or low hill rising from the meadows. Half-close your eyes and imagine the lane, the meadows, and all else below the promontory as water, and you can see why the Romans chose it as a base and haven when they made their permanent invasion in AD 43. A hundred years before, Caesar had come and gone. Now, under his descendant, Claudius, they were back to stay. This promontory into the Stour estuary was not only deserted, unlike the cliffs of Dover, but offered a harbour for ships and easy access to the interior.

From the lane a track leads to the walls of the fort built at *Portus Rutupiae*. So important had it been that a huge triumphal arch had been erected, to mark Rome's gateway to Britannia; the cruciform base of it remains. But the same danger that brought the army to Dover in 270 to build a new fort there, raids by Saxon pirates, caused them to break down the great monument and re-use its material in the walls of another Fort of the Saxon Shore. Like its fellow forts, which lined south-eastern Britannia, it was not built as well as most earlier Roman construc-tions, the stones of all shapes and sizes thrown together, bound by strong mortar. The walls here, still 20 feet high in places, are of this material.

You can either return to the A257 by the same way, or if you feel like some entertainment, you can follow the lane farther on, taking the first turning left and experiencing all the thrills of negotiating a typical marsh road. Never more than 10 feet wide, it winds about like the trail of a drunk. Eventually it reaches the A257 and you **Ash** are on a more sober course for Ash, whose church spire you have seen from the windy levels. You are on the ridge that separates the Stour valley from the interior farmland, with **Wingham** orchards and arable fields. Wingham has a wide street with antique shops and restaurants and, as the road turns sharply right by the churchyard, four ancient houses, two of which are inns, which once comprised a canonry established in the late thirteenth century. The ridge road **Littlebourne** passes through Littlebourne on the Little Stour, which is the Nailbourne supplemented by a spring, and 2 miles farther on, instead of going straight back to Canterbury, you might take the last diversion of the tour by turning right to **Fordwich** Fordwich, reached by taking the first turning left after passing Canterbury's golf course.

A steep descent from the pine-crowned ridge down the High Street arrives at right angles to the river, which is the chief reason for so small a village to be distinguished as a 'town'. When the Stour was deeper and wider, and higher up unnavigable, Fordwich could provide wharfage for ships carrying goods to and from Canterbury. It acquired rights of self-government, with a mayor, a charter, and its own Town Hall, by the river, with an antiquated crane attached for unloading ships. It even became a 'limb' of the Cinque Port Sandwich, to help pay for the ships it had to build. The little church, with high box-pews, is filled with the town's departed glories – yet it still has a mayor and uses the Town Hall.

To return to Canterbury you need only cross the old brick bridge across the Stour, go to the end of the lane and turn left on the A28.

Rye

Tourist Information Office
Council Offices, Ferry Road, tel 2293

Population 4,370

Museums
Ypres Tower Cinque Ports Museum
Cherries Folk Museum, Playden (by appointment)

Places of Interest
Church of St Mary the Virgin   Mermaid Street
Town Hall   Flushing Inn
Landgate   Lamb House
Ypres Tower   Rye Town Model

A fortified hill-town is unusual in England. Rye used to be an island (hence its name, *Atte-ar-eye*, at the island, in old English) in the tidal estuaries of three rivers, Rother, Tillingham, and Brede, which issue from the hills to north and west. As a rising fishing and trading port it was added to the Cinque Ports Federation in King John's time (early thirteenth century) and thereafter enjoyed the same privileges, for the same duties, as the rest. It suffered as much financially from the strains of the long wars against the French, but more physically, as it was sacked and burned twice, in 1378 and 1448. However, the continuing prosperity of its burgesses can be seen in the wealth of building of stout houses into the nineteenth century, although it was no longer an active port. Its unique charm has exerted a magnetic attraction to writers and artists.

The chief entrance to the town in the fourteenth-century protective walls, little of which remain, is the Landgate. Passing between its drum towers and beneath its deep archway, you climb into the eastern end of the High Street, but leave it by the first turning left, East Street, which brings you into Market Street, passing a house on the left corner where the painter Paul Nash once lived. Ancient houses abound, such as the *Flushing Inn*, now a fine restaurant, next to the Town Hall, a pillared building of 1742. Between the two a very narrow cobbled street takes you into the topmost, innermost, and rarest quarter, Church Square. On all sides a diversity of historic houses face the churchyard. At the far end of the eastern side of the square, overlooking the estuary and the sea, is a miniature castle called Ypres or Baddings Tower, which was built in the mid-thirteenth century for the town's protection. Below it is a pleasant terrace called the Gun-garden, with newly cast cannons, of somewhat dubious military value. Along the south side of the square, interspersed with houses of all ages, are a Methodist chapel, the stone gable of what used to be a chapel of Carmelite friars, and, in Watchbell Street, a new Catholic church.

Watchbell Street, named from the alarm bell once kept there, ends abruptly with a precipitous drop to the wharves by the Tillingham river and the levels to the west. The *Hope Anchor Hotel* fronts the sheer cliff; a path through its yard and little Trader's Passage will bring you to the lower end of Mermaid Street and a quick descent to the quayside.

On the right is a building which houses a model of the town and a *Son et Lumière* display to go with it, showing daily. If you now go up Mermaid Street, which is cobbled like all these topmost streets, you will see more timbered houses such as the Old Hospital, and near the top the famous *Mermaid Inn*, an extraordinary building dating from the fifteenth century. Sharp right at the top you find Lamb House, a brick Georgian place where the American writer Henry James lived.

Return down West Street now to the High Street, turn right and see, opposite the eighteenth-century *George Hotel*, the dark red brick with projecting pilasters of Peacocke's Grammar School (no longer in academic use) of the early seventeenth century. Turn right at the *George Hotel* corner, back to Market Street and the church tower and entrance, over which two gilded oaken boys strike the quarter on the sixteenth-century clock. The church is high, light, calm, and tranquil, although full of reminders of Rye's tempestuous and violent past.

Rye has plenty of good hotels and a multitude of antique, art, and gift shops. It also has its own pottery and iron foundry, and gives an impression of thriving prosperity.

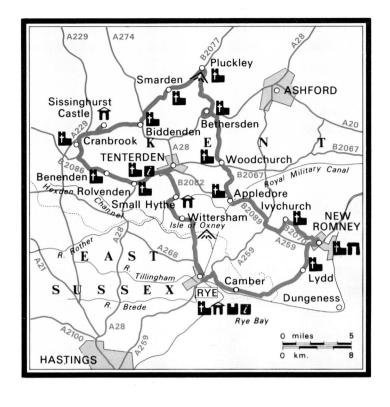

Rye – Lydd – New Romney – Appledore – Bethersden – Pluckley – Biddenden – Sissinghurst Castle – Cranbrook – Benenden – Rolvenden – Tenterden – Smallhythe – Wittersham – Rye

Tour length 66 miles

Diversity of landscape is the keynote to this tour, from the bewildering complexity of the marshes, crossed by innumerable watercourses, to the lush wooded hills and vales of the Weald. The curious linking factor is that all this largely pastoral land has been artificially created: that on the marsh, from tidal mud-flats, and that in the hills, from dense and hitherto impenetrable forest. Here in this tour in south-western Kent can be seen the patient, long-term impact of man, mindful of his necessities, on his environment.

The Marsh is hard to understand until you look at a map and see where the hills come to an edge and a number of rivers and streams issue from them. Add to them the action of the sea in depositing quantities of shingle, and the picture begins to emerge. The towns, Rye, Lydd and New Romney, began their existence as islands, based partly on shingle banks: all were sea-ports. Behind them, between Lydd and Romney and the hills, were lagoons, supplied by the rivers and filled by the sea at high tide. Over the years, starting in Roman times, efforts were made to win back the lagoons from the sea for cultivation. First the easternmost part, Romney Marsh proper, was won and walled in. The A259 today travels along the top of this wall, called Rhee (water) Wall. The River Rother then issued alongside it to emerge at the sea at New Romney. After a great storm in 1287 it changed course to Rye and the reclaiming of the land between Rye and the Rhee Wall, now called Walland (Wall-land) Marsh, was possible. It is very low-lying, full of drainage ditches and streams, and is excellent pasturage for sheep, the wool from which is the key to the Marsh's prosperity.

Camber — Take the A259 towards New Romney from Rye, but turn right on the B2975 at East Guldeford, on the way to Camber and Lydd. Camber, sheltering from the sea behind a sand-dune sea-wall, consists principally of golf courses and caravans, and the lane, passing between the green pastures of the marsh and the gravelly wilderness of Dungeness's shingle bank, makes for Lydd, whose church tower can be seen long before it is reached. The former importance of a place can often be guessed by the size of its oldest building, which in most cases is the parish church. Lydd's is sometimes called 'the Cathedral of the Marshes', and evidence of Saxon, pre-Conquest material in the north-west walls shows that Lydd was a thriving port on its shingle island until the fateful 1287 storm. In 1940 the chancel was bombed, but it has been rebuilt most skilfully.

The road winds across the windy, airy fields to New Romney, hardest hit of all by the storm. A short way to the north-west is Old Romney, but in fact neither antedates the other: there were three churches to serve a large parish, and the adjectives merely distinguish them. The third, Hope All Saints, became redundant and lies in **New Romney** ruins. New Romney had a harbour on the Rother estuary and was one of the original Cinque Ports. Its street is wide and lined even now with inns, restaurants, and shops, the majority of which post-date 1287 and testify to the marsh's other source of wealth: wool. The church, in a side street to the right, is a splendid example of Romanesque eleventh-century church architecture. Two reminders of the extent of the damage from that frightful night in 1287 can be seen: first, the church is lower than the road, because so much debris was thrown up that the former level was never regained; second, the massive pillars of the nave still show faint discolouration, marking the level of the flood-waters – not on the octagonal chancel pillars, however, since they were added in the fourteenth century.

Railway enthusiasts have two treats in store on this tour. If you go past Church Street and turn right on the B2071 road, you can quickly find the New Romney station on the Romney, Hythe, and Dymchurch Railway, which is a miniature railway with working steam locomotives drawing real passenger carriages, and running a regular service.

Opposite the end of Church Street the B2070

road may take you on its tortuous way between the dykes and sheep-pastures to a small corner of Romney Marsh proper (east of the Rhee Wall). On your right you can see the jagged ruins of Hope All Saints. All around are the apparently illimitable levels, dotted with the white blobs of sheep and the flash of water. The only sounds (if you stop your motor) are those of the sheep and the skylarks. Overhead stretches the vast inverted bowl of sky, as at sea, from horizon to horizon: the quality of light here is intense, almost luminous.

Ivychurch   Ivychurch, on this road, has a church far bigger than its size seems to warrant: another testimony to the depth of the sheep-farmers' purses. It has a two-storey porch, whose upper floor used to be the village school. Despite the French wars of the fourteenth century which came near to ruining the Cinque Ports, the trade in raw wool was evidently still good: the church dates from the 1360s.

Turn left on a lane close by the inn, and experience, even briefly, the quiet pleasures of a genuine Marsh road. It is unlikely that you will meet anyone here, except perhaps a marsh shepherd. Before long the lane emerges on the Rhee Wall opposite the A259's departure from it towards Rye. Turn right, on the Wall road, now called the B2080, through Brenzett, then Snargate, and make for Appledore. You cross the Dowels, one of the last, and lowest-lying, parts of the Marsh to be reclaimed. You cross also the railway (the full-sized one) and the Royal Military Canal, which runs along the whole length of the northern side of the Marsh and was intended, when built by the order of the Prime Minister, William Pitt, in 1804, to act as a moat, a line of defence, to slow down the invading French *Grande Armée*. It never came, and neither did the German army of 1940, although new gun positions were built along the canal in case it did.

As you cross the bridge over the canal you leave
Appledore   the Marsh, for Appledore is on the lowest of the hills. There are two good inns on the right of the wide street, which contains an attractive assortment of houses, and near the first, at the

churchyard gate, is a large notice telling the village's history. The church itself is on an artificially raised earthwork which appears to have been constructed by a marauding Viking army in the 890s as a base camp. It took King Alfred the Great five years to dislodge them.

Woodchurch If, instead of following the B2080 as it swings left north of Appledore, you fork right, following the signposts to Woodchurch, you can enjoy the first of the day's changes of scenery, for you will have exchanged the Marsh's wide open airiness for dense woodland, and its flatness for gently undulating hills. The lane emerges on the B2067 road, and it is essential to turn right off this almost at once, to get to the green and church of Woodchurch, both of which are worth a visit. The green looks like anyone's cherished memory of a typical English village: an open grassy space with children playing, fringed by tall trees, an inviting inn or two, and some venerable timber-framed cottages, the church spire completing the skyline. After passing the church at the top of the village, turn right, making for Bethersden. The hills are now steeper, like an increasingly rougher sea, and arable fields appear among the green pastures, but the overall impression is still of woodland.

You are on the edge of a stretch of country, measuring from east to west nearly a hundred miles, which until fairly late in the Middle Ages was dense forest, with a very small permanent population. From the seventh century on, clearings were made for pasturing pigs by the inhabitants of northern and eastern Kent, the population centres. The clearings, called *dens*, belonged to certain parishes in those areas, and each year the pigs would be driven into them to fatten up ready for slaughter in late November. The forest was called the Weald.

Bethersden Bethersden, where this lane takes you when you have arrived at the main A28 road and turned left, was one of these clearings at first, but like many others developed a permanent settlement with its own church. To the west of the village on the A28 is the *Bull Inn*, where splendid refreshment may be found.

Lanes lead off the A28 into the village, which

Mermaid Street, Rye

has the typical Wealden mixture of timber-frame, brick, and weatherboard (overlapping horizontal wooden boards), with tiled roofs. Nearby was a quarry from which the polished stone, known as Bethersden Marble, was in much demand for memorials. On one lane out of the village is an old farmhouse called *Lovelace*, part of which is a fragment from the home of the seventeenth-century Royalist poet of that name.

If you go to the end of Bethersden's street past the church and turn left, you can find lanes to Pluckley, through choppy hilly country full of woods and green fields and any number of oast houses, mostly converted for private habitation. The proper function of an oast, which is a kind of two-storey barn with one or more conical-roofed towers, is for drying (in the towers, which are kilns) and storing the flowers of the hop plant, whose fragrance is used for flavouring beer. The plant is grown less than formerly, so the oasts, found all over Kent, are often now adapted as houses.

Pluckley Pluckley is on the edge of the Weald, on the Chart Hills which extend as a ridge from Ashford to Maidstone and beyond. One salient feature of Pluckley that you may notice is that every cottage built not later than the nineteenth century has the same kind of windows, round-topped in narrow pairs, threes, or even fours. The entire parish used to belong to the land-owning family of Dering, who lived at their manor-house nearby called Surrenden Dering, now vanished. A romantic-minded squire, Sir Edward Dering, who lived through all but eleven years of the nineteenth century, knowing the legend that an ancestor escaped from Parliamentary forces in the Civil War by climbing through just such a window, wished to commemorate it by changing every window of every cottage on his estate. Most have never changed back.

In the little square by the churchyard there is a venerable inn, the *Black Horse*, reputedly haunted, parts of which date from the fifteenth century (all parts with Dering windows, of course). Opposite an avenue of cottages leads to the churchyard gate.

If you turn left on the B2077 road from the *Black*

Horse, you dip steeply down to the Weald again, among the trees, passing a number of oasts, and many old timbered houses, some subsequently **Smarden** bricked on the outside and tiled on top. Smarden is full of them. Beware of the sharp zig-zag turns which carry the road round Smarden's church-yard. The road crosses the little River Beult and takes you to the A274 road. Turn left on it, then **Biddenden** right into the main street of Biddenden, and there you will find more timbered houses, one of them a tea-shop of national repute. Nearby there is also a Cloth Hall, a workshop for weavers of the wool industry which, as in the marsh, was a major source of wealth. Look at the right-hand side of the street going towards the church, at the pavement: it is of stone flags, and was the pack-pony path in wool-trading days.

You are now on the A262 road, which dodges the churchyard, as at Smarden, and delves into yet more thickly wooded country, up and down steeper hills, at the far side of which there is a **Sissinghurst** well-signposted lane to Sissinghurst Castle. It is open daily except Mondays during the summer and it is worth visiting, not for the castle, but for the gardens. It never was a proper castle, but comprises fragments of three successive manor-houses on the site during some four hundred years. In 1930 when quite ruinous, the estate was bought by Sir Harold and Lady Nicolson (the writer Vita Sackville-West) and restored to order. They created the gardens out of the wilderness, and the National Trust continues to tend their refreshing beauty.

Although you may leave this small Arcady with difficulty, you might return to the A262, go from this to the A229, turning left, and left again on **Cranbrook** the B2189 road into Cranbrook, where houses are mainly Wealden weatherboard, there is a large school, a stately church, and a big windmill which until recently was in full business milling corn. Continuing past the mill, up and over the **Benenden** hill, you can then fork right for Benenden, meeting the B2086 and turning left on it. Soon after passing the entrance to Benenden School, you may like to pause for a while at the green, for here as at Woodchurch is the archetypal English village scene, especially if a game of cricket is in progress. On the skyline is the church, trees flank the two sides, on one corner an inn, across the road on the fourth side the little post office and an old house which used to be a school.

Rolvenden   On your way to Rolvenden you pass two more windmills, one severely decayed on your left, the other freshly restored. Rolvenden is grouped around a T-junction with the main A28 road, so traffic tends to be heavy, but this cannot detract from its pleasing street. In the church there is a private pew for the local manor-house family consisting of an entire room, with its own fireplace.

The A28 will take you to Tenterden. As the road dips into the valley of the Newmill Channel, one of the streams that feed the marsh dykes, it crosses a railway, with Rolvenden station on your right. This is the second offering for railway fans, for this is a life-sized toy railway, the resurrected Kent and East Sussex, by and for those who like playing around with trains. The assembled rolling stock and steam engines themselves constitute a railway museum.

Tenterden   Up the hill into Tenterden you find a wide, stately High Street full of elegant shops, houses, inns, and restaurants, all the trappings of a Wealden metropolis. There is a Town Hall next to the ancient *Woolpack Inn*, displaying the coat of arms of the Cinque Ports Federation. In the troubled days of the Hundred Years' War, Tenterden was attached to Rye. Tenterden is now 20 miles from the sea, but if you take the B2082 road southward from the High Street you may see what ships had to do with a wool-trading town.

This road dips gradually to some low-lying land
Smallhythe   with a village called Smallhythe. A hythe, as in the town near Folkestone, is a harbour, a wharf; this, therefore, used to be a harbour, the one that served Tenterden, which rendered Tenterden suitable for assistance to Rye. There is no visible water now other than a narrow, shallow stream called the Reading Sewer, but in the Middle Ages there was a wide tidal channel which stretched from the Rother estuary, even after the 1287 storm, and surrounded the lump of land visible across the levels opposite Smallhythe, known as

the Isle of Oxney. Guided by the tall church tower of Tenterden, which stands high on the ridge above the little port, ships could make safe anchorage and secure a valuable cargo of wool.

All the present buildings of Smallhythe were built after 1514, because in that year the whole place burned down by accident. The harbour-master's house was put up soon after this disaster, and because the great actress Ellen Terry spent her last years in it, has been preserved as a museum with all her relics. Even to the non-theatrically minded, the opportunity for seeing inside such a timbered sixteenth-century cottage justifies a visit.

You still have to cross water to reach Oxney, even if it is only the Reading Sewer and the bridge is small, but if you follow the road up to the long, low, whale-backed ridge and look out over the levels on either side, it is not difficult to imagine them all water, the sheep as boats, and Oxney an island again. Wittersham is its chief village, and where the road turns by another windmill and runs steeply down to the Rother, look back and see how much Oxney has the look and feel of an island. The road, climbing from the level to the ridge of Iden, takes you straight back to Rye.

Wittersham

Hastings

Tourist Information Office
4 Robertson Terrace, tel 424242

Population 72,170

Theatres
White Rock Pavilion
Stables Theatre, High Street

Cinema
Classic, Queen's Road

Museums
Museum and Art Gallery, Cambridge Road
Museum of Local History, High Street
Fishermen's Museum, Rock-a-Nore Road

Places of Interest

St Clement's Church   St Clement's Caves
High Street   Castle
The Stade   Hastings Embroidery

Divided by Castle Hill as if by the Berlin Wall, Hastings is in
two distinct parts. To the west is the holiday resort, with all the
necessary hotels, shops, pier, entertainments of various kinds,
railway and bus stations, and streets of residential flats and
houses. To the east, in the narrow defile between Castle and
East Hills, lies the old Hastings, the basis of its long history as
one of the original Cinque Ports.

The Caves give an indication of the length of time in which
some form of habitation has existed here, the castle its
defensive importance. William the Conqueror put up one of his
temporary wooden strongholds on the hill, and the present
ruins are of its replacement. The astonishing, close-set assembly of weathered houses tumbled in the narrow cleft
between the two hills, set in three main streets and criss-
crossed by innumerable passages, alleys, stairways, and side-
streets, shows the tenacious endurance of the little town's will
to survive. The old Town Hall, a blue-painted Georgian edifice
in the High Street, houses a museum illustrating this tradition.
Out of so many extraordinary examples it is hard to pick any in
particular of these delightful little town houses, but the Old
Pump House in George Street, and Pulpitt Gate at the end of
All Saints Street should not be missed.

The whole town is permeated with the fresh, strong, salty, fishy atmosphere of its primary reason for existence, and on the front, east of the funfair, beneath East Cliff, still stand some of the tall dark-stained weatherboarded drying sheds for the fishermen's nets. Fishing boats are pulled up on the beach and their owners stand ready to sell their morning's catch. Gulls wheel screaming overhead, diving for scraps. The battered remnant of the old harbour pier butts brokenly into the sea. The funicular carriage grinds slowly up East Hill above, the multiplicity of sea-front pubs begin to open their doors. Climb up and down the twisting stepped passages, passing intriguing courts and tiny squares between the sprucely-kept houses; visit St Clement's Church, between two levels of streets; sniff the tangy air as you enter the Fishermen's Chapel and museum, down on the Stade, among the mewing, diving sea-birds and the old drying-sheds: this is the Hastings that will enthral you and tempt your return.

Hastings beach

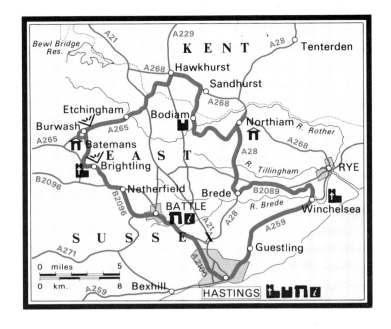

Hastings – Battle – Brightling – Burwash – Hawkhurst – Bodiam – Northiam – Brede – Winchelsea – Hastings

Tour length 55 miles

This is one of the shortest tours in the book, but as it includes so much to see, it could develop, paradoxically, into one of the longest. Tucked away in some of the loveliest countryside in south-east England, with Wealden woodland pasture, deep valleys, and high hills, and the green levels of marshland, you will find many treasures. There is the best-known battlefield in all English history, crowned by the ruins of the great monastery and by the little town that both took their names from it; two beautiful but not immense houses, both typical of the area in entirely different ways, and one of them set in a garden as near to perfection as makes little difference; a medieval castle which looks like an illustration from one of Sir Walter Scott's novels; and another of the fascinating Cinque Ports. All these, and more, can be found within this short compass.

From Hastings take the A2100 road along the ridge to Telham and Battle. This is the way that Duke William of Normandy took, with his bold, almost foolhardy little force of Normans, Bretons, and Frenchmen, in October 1066, in his desperate enterprise to capture a rich and **Telham** populous kingdom. Telham is the hill where he set up his standard, somewhere among these modern bungalows. Opposite him, on Senlac Hill across the shallow valley of the little Brede stream, King Harold assembled his troops and dug in behind their palisade, a formidable obstacle.

The conflict was fierce and sanguinary, the outcome decisive for Duke William and the history of England. On Senlac Hill the victor caused a great monastic abbey to be built, in **Battle** thanksgiving for his success, and called it Battle Abbey. Around it, to serve it, a little town grew, its name permanently commemorating that October day. The town has outlived the abbey:

except for its gateway, which was the last part of it to be built, it is in ruins. A house, now a girls' school, was built from the materials after the Dissolution, and the remaining structure above ground may be inspected, any day of the week and most of the day. Much has been newly excavated and discovered, and the view over the battlefield from the English position may excite the imagination.

There is an excellent little museum in the tile-hung Georgian Langton House, in the High Street, the town's social centre, on the right from the Abbey Gate. Apart from more recent relics it has a copy of the famous Bayeux Tapestry, with some sections authentically woven, telling the whole invasion story, and a model panorama of the battle, offering easier understanding of how the action fitted into the landscape. The High Street, which widens at the Abbey Gate for what was once a market place with a bull-ring set in the ground, but now, inevitably, is a car park, is full of mainly Georgian houses, although, as in many English country towns, some of the houses are much older than their eighteenth-century brick façades. One quite undisguised is the *Pilgrims' Rest*, a medieval hall-house (timber-framed, with floor open to the ceiling-rafters in the centre) close by the Abbey Gate, which still functions as a place of refreshment for travellers.

At the far end of the High Street beyond the modern market, take the left turning, the A269 road, for a short distance, forking right on the Netherfield B2096 to Netherfield, through the woods of the extensive Ashburnham estate. A little beyond Netherfield, at the bottom of a steep hill called Darwell Hole, turn off right on a lane which carries you into the densest of woodland and remotest of pasturages, as if untouched since the Weald was first cleared by the intrepid swine-herds: to an unheard-of hamlet called Cackle Street, and at last to the brilliant heights of Brightling.

Brightling Brightling village and the ridge on which it stands are full of reminders of its most celebrated squire, Jack Fuller, a mighty man who occupied for many years a seat in the House of Commons, and now, reputedly, one for ever in the huge pyramid-tomb in the churchyard. There is a classical temple in his park, an obelisk and an observatory on a nearby eminence, and a false church-spire on a hill, placed there merely to improve the view: all at Fuller's instigation.

The view, especially to the north, is engrossing and entrancing: as Kipling put it,

'Belt upon belt, the wooded
Dim blue goodness of the Weald.'

Rudyard Kipling had cause to know what he was describing, because he lived nearby. From Brightling take the turning left, across the observatory-crowned eminence and through a leafy green roller-coaster kind of lane, up and down (usually unencumbered by any other traffic) until you run up a final ridge to the village of Burwash. Go left along its street and left again, guided by the sign 'Batemans'. This narrow lane takes you back into the valley you have just quit, to the beautiful old stone house which was Kipling's home from 1902 until he died in 1936.

Burwash

As a Wealden ironmaster's house of 1634, a time when iron-founding, from the abundant iron-stone everywhere, with furnaces fuelled with limitless timber, was a principal industry in the Weald, Bateman's itself is a classic example. Kipling's presence in the house for so long gave it his imprint and left his mementoes. It is open every day except Fridays during the summer.

Burwash itself, stretched out on its ridge like Battle, is full of interest, with houses reflecting the opulence of iron-smelting days. The Romans smelted iron in the Weald, and the industry was resumed in the later Middle Ages, reaching a resounding zenith in the sixteenth and seventeenth centuries, when cannon and shot were supplied for use against England's enemies, not to mention against other Englishmen in the Civil War. By this time the consumption of forest timber had reached a rate that alarmed the Admiralty in case of shortage of ship-building timber. Coke was developed instead and in time the Weald's industry died.

The A265 road going eastward from Burwash takes you through typically Wealden, thickly wooded country down to the Rother valley and

Etchingham across the railway at Etchingham, and up into
Hawkhurst Kent again to Hawkhurst. Inns catering for
hungry and thirsty travellers abound: the
Admiral Vernon at Burwash, the *Etchingham
Arms*, the *Eight Bells* here at Hawkhurst are
three out of many. Hawkhurst is a bipartite
village, part round the church and green, where
the *Eight Bells* stands, and part on the next hill
called Highgate, where there are shops and more
inns. Hawkhurst had a terrible smuggling connection in the eighteenth century, as it was the
headquarters of a violent and vicious gang which
controlled the entire neighbourhood with a
Mafiosi mixture of bribery and brutishness, using
the desolate coastline of Romney Marsh to run
its highly profitable cargoes of brandy, tobacco,
and lace.

At Highgate you meet the A268 road: turn right
and you can go with it as it follows the ridge
between the Rother and one of its tributaries, the
Sandhurst Hexden Channel. At Sandhurst you will see on
Bodiam the right a lane signposted Bodiam, and this will
take you down from the ridge among the wooded
slopes to the village of that name by the Rother,
and opposite the *Castle Inn* you can turn into the
immense car park provided for visitors to Bodiam
Castle.

The walk is not long. On your right the Rother
flows between its raised banks; across the sheep-
pasture before you, beyond the few trees, you can
see the creamy walls and turrets rearing high
above the placid waters of the moat. It looks like
a perfect, miraculously preserved medieval
castle, towered and battlemented, complete in its
wide moat. Preserved it is, but perfect it is not,
for although the curtain walls and their towers
and gatehouses are intact, little remains within
them of the hall, kitchens, and domestic apartments but their foundations, low walls, and
chimneys.

Bodiam was built in the 1380s, at the same time
as Canterbury's and Rye's walls, and for the
same reason, fear of French invasion. It guarded
the navigable Rother, but was never tested,
never involved in any military action, and
gradually fell into ruin. However, you can climb
up the spiral steps to the towers, and imagine

scenes which might have taken place if the French had come.

A hump-backed bridge carries the road over the Rother, and there is then the level crossing of the Kent and East Sussex Railway, whose Bodiam station is adjacent, with trains to Tenterden. Up the hill past the station, turn off left to Ewhurst and Northiam: this lane takes you along the southern ridge of the Rother valley, above hop-gardens, among oasts and tile-hung cottages **Northiam** bright with flowers. Both villages, Northiam the larger, are pretty, but at the northern end of Northiam, on the edge of a ridge with a wide sweeping view of the Rother valley and the **Great Dixter** greeny-blue wooded hills beyond, is Great Dixter. A superb fifteenth-century timbered house, rescued from ruin in 1911 by Nathaniel Lloyd and restored by the architect Sir Edwin Lutyens, it has a great hall, open from floor to timbered ceiling, and the traditional medieval solar at one end. It has some exquisite furniture by Chippendale, Hepplewhite, and Sheraton, and tapestries and other needlework, some of it by the Lloyd family which still owns the house. The immaculately tended gardens are famous; on a sunny summer afternoon they epitomise all that is understood by an English country garden. There is that superb natural colour-blend unrealisable by artificial means, but available each year from the season's flowers; the small movement of bees and butterflies, the faint hum of other insects and only birdsong otherwise to disturb the tranquillity; the hundred and one scents blending in the fragrant air.

From Great Dixter you can return to the A28 through Northiam and go towards Hastings until **Brede** you reach the pleasant village of Brede. A turning from it leads to the B2089 road which occupies the ridge between the Brede and Tillingham rivers, but when you have passed **Udimore** through Udimore take a lane to the right to Winchelsea. The going is slightly hazardous because the lane is narrow and wriggly, but as it drops to the levels of the Brede river it should effect the feeling of transition from the forested Wealden hill country to the estuary marshes. If you can risk taking your eye off the road for an instant, you can see ahead the high promontory on which Winchelsea stands, and in the distance just visible is the church-capped pyramid of Rye.

Your lane turns right across the Brede and the railway, and climbs very steeply round a hairpin bend to the height, passing the little Landgate. By the standards of South-East England, Winchelsea is a new town. Originally it occupied a low island in the estuary of the rivers, like Rye but not so prominent, consisting probably mainly of shingle. It became a thriving port and contributed fully to the Cinque Ports' duties. A great storm in 1250 ruined it, then the yet more disastrous tempest of 1287 destroyed it, but King Edward I had already authorised its rebuilding on this promontory. The regularity of its grid of streets, like any planned town from the days of the Roman Empire to those of the United States of America, proclaims its pedigree. Once more it gained strength and prosperity, only to be ruined anew by two factors: the French wars with their colossal financial burden, worsened by destruction by French raiding parties, and the gradual recession of the sea from its harbour, leaving the town stranded.

Winchelsea is immensely attractive, its amply-proportioned handsome houses suggesting that, like Rye, the gap left by the absence of maritime trade was filled by the munificence of local sheep, but its church remains as the French left it, with the chancel and two side chapels standing and in use and the rest in ruins. The medieval stone Town Hall is the museum, there are some other buildings, like the Armoury, which survive from its earliest days, and the fortified Strand Gate straddles perilously the road to Rye. The atmosphere is quite different from Rye's: it seems calm, serene, acquiescent in , the permanent departure of importance, without the same urgency. Other than agriculture, there is no attempt at modern industry. If Rye is still anxious to look young and keep fit, Winchelsea has gracefully accepted respectable retirement.

The A259 road, which shoots the narrows of the Strand Gate, has to zig-zag around the grid-plan, but will then assist you back through Icklesham and Guestling to Hastings.

Winchelsea

Tunbridge Wells

Tourist Information Office
Town Hall, Mount Pleasant Road, tel 26121

Population 45,000

Theatre
Assembly Hall, Crescent Road

Cinema
Classic, Mount Pleasant Road

Museum
Town Museum, Public Library

Places of Interest

Pantiles	Church of King Charles Martyr
Chalybeate spring	High Rocks

The town of Tunbridge Wells is spread about a deep wooded valley in a somewhat haphazard fashion, and owes its existence to the discovery in 1606 that the water from a certain spring in the Earl of Abergavenny's estate could cure all kinds of ailment. The spring was chalybeate, impregnated with the iron from the local stone. The earl enclosed the spring, and before long a succession of high society sufferers from their over-loaded constitutions came to escape from London's plague-ridden streets each summer and refresh themselves. One George Nash, in the early eighteenth century, alternating between Bath and these Tunbridge Wells, master of ceremonies in both spas, created the desirably elegant atmosphere, and it is from these departed glories that the town derives its historical centre.

It is therefore the area about the Pump Room to which you must go for the best of Tunbridge Wells: the splendid colonnade, the shady trees, the tiled walk, the minstrels' gallery, the shops, tea-rooms, taverns, and coffee-houses, the graceful houses, all of this now known as the Pantiles. At their end, beyond the Pump Room, where the queer tasting water still bubbles up, there is the church built in 1678 and dedicated to King Charles the Martyr (martyr for what cause, one wonders?) in stately classical style.

The popularity of the Wells in the eighteenth century brought prosperity to the growing town, which soon offered plenty of hotels and genteel lodgings for the seasonal visitors. Up on

Mount Ephraim, for example, on the western bank of the valley, a row of large, fashionable residences arose, along with the vast *Wellington Hotel*. Set out before them, the spacious and wooded Royal Common sweeps down to London Road and the Pantiles, well above the common throng down in the valley. The latter, with the town's further development, was vastly augmented when the railway was built in the mid-nineteenth century, and it is from this date that the remainder of the town began to grow.

Modern Tunbridge Wells is large, has manufacturing industries, shops, stores, still plenty of hotels, and its Assembly Hall where symphony orchestras play from time to time. It has sports fields and the extensive commons, and there in the centre of things, the marvellous elegance of the Pantiles.

The Pantiles, Tunbridge Wells

Tunbridge Wells – Groombridge – Penshurst – Chiddingstone – Hever – Hartfield – Ashdown Forest – Uckfield – Mayfield – Lamberhurst – Tunbridge Wells

Tour length 60 miles

The Earl of Abergavenny could have made little of his chalybeate spring if his estate had been, say, in mid-Devonshire, or Norfolk, or, as his title implies, in South Wales. The exploitation of such a resource depended on accessibility from some large population centre, the bigger the better: what more promising than London itself? The success of Tunbridge Wells, in fact, is no more than a reflection of much of this beautiful area, so long a part of the vast impenetrable Weald. It is within reach of London, even by horse and carriage and on the vilest of roads. From opulent city merchants to social-climbing knights like Sir Thomas Bullen, they chose to build their palaces within forty miles of London. Would King Henry VIII have pursued Sir Thomas's daughter quite so attentively if he had had to follow her home to Northumberland?

So the great houses proliferated in West Kent and North Sussex, and the Wealden trees obligingly swallowed them up, screening them from one another, giving the required impression of remote rusticity. They still do, even now when so many more refugees from the capital have made their dormitory homes among them. In this tour we shall see more of *rus* than *urbs*, despite this migration.

The A264 road runs along Mount Ephraim, the 'right' quarter of Tunbridge Wells, due west through part of the all-embracing forest to the **Rusthall Common** hamlet at Rusthall Common, where the sandstone outcrops, and erosion has shaped a monstrous toad out of one such rock. From the Common a lane leads off left, diving steeply down into the valley and the trees, and at the bottom a cliff rears high above on your left, with a funicular lift to fetch you up to another stone outcrop, utilised by Iron Age Celts as a fort and called High Rocks.

   Drive on through the forest, dark and mysterious, cool and menacing, until you cross the

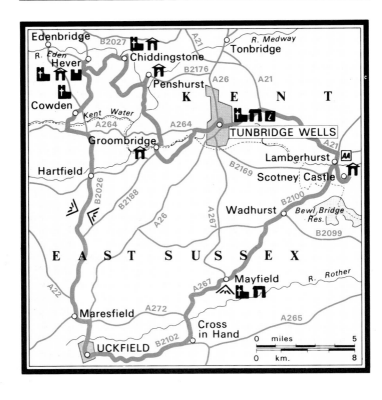

railway for the second time and come to the pretty village of Groombridge, back on your A264 road. There is a triangular green surrounded by terraced cottages of the period when the neighbouring Wells were attracting dyspeptic stomachs by the score from London, and on the road is a little brick chapel with a big Perpendicular window and a clock dated 1792 (added at least 100 years later). A stream called the Kent Water flows along this valley, beneath the bluff of High Rocks, acting as the boundary between Kent and Sussex: as it bisects Groombridge the parish is in both counties. From the chapel a footpath leads through a field to Groombridge Place, which is just in Kent; most of its park is in Sussex. The house is a small Restoration-style manor-house, on an ancient moated site long in the possession of the Waller family. Three hundred years have mellowed the rose-red bricks, the high-pitched roof, and the colonnaded entrance porch, and the vivid, verdant lawns, trees, rhododendrons, the high forested setting, all have laid claim to this created artifice as part of the natural landscape.

From the green at Groombridge we must appear to return along the A264 towards Tunbridge Wells, up the steep northern bank of the Kent Water valley; but soon, at the top, take the B2188 left to Penshurst. The dense forest-land rises and dips into sudden ravines, passes Ashurst Park and through Fordcombe, crosses the infant Medway, and twists up its western bank to Penshurst.

Penshurst

The word *hurst* means settlement in the woods; the manor is an old one. Sir Stephen de Penchester, Lord Warden of the Cinque Ports under Edward I, held it in the thirteenth century. In 1338 his descendants sold it to Sir John de Pulteney, a rich city merchant, four times Lord Mayor of London. It passed through the hands of Henry V's brothers the Dukes of Bedford and Gloucester, three successive Dukes of Buckingham, and the Crown. Finally young Edward VI granted it in 1552 to Sir William Sidney, whose descendants still live there.

The Place is a combination of Pulteney's great hall and solar, Bedford's apartments, and the Sidneys' additions and amendments. The necessities of this tour mean that, regrettably, it is probably reached before it is open to the public at one o'clock; however it is worth a journey from Tunbridge Wells for its own sake. The grounds are extensive, the village and its Sidney-filled church are of customary Wealden character, and there are admirable views all around, with the River Medway flowing at the bottom of the hill.

Chiddingstone

To reach Chiddingstone from Penshurst means an excursion into the lanes and is not easy. From Penshurst return along the B2188 in the direction of Fordcombe; go first right after crossing the river, right again to Chiddingstone Hoath, right again at Hoath Corner, and finally left into Chiddingstone itself. All the way, you are in dense woodland and pasture, as you would expect in the Weald. The little street of Chiddingstone, all on one side facing the churchyard, consists of a string of splendid old houses, mainly of the sixteenth and seventeenth centuries, including a fine timbered range called Porch House, and ending at the corner with the tile-hung *Castle Inn* of great repute. The Castle, whose gates confront the end of the street, was built by the Streatfeild family in picturesque eighteenth-century Gothic.

There are more lanes to negotiate to reach Hever: bear left when you have swung round the corner past Chiddingstone Church and the Castle gate, ignoring the right turning, then take the next turning right, down into the River Eden valley; go right at the Edenbridge road at the bottom, and first right off that to Hever. No help may be gained by distant views of church spires, because you are in close, high woods all the way. By the *Henry VIII* inn there is a car park, and as the road turns sharply round the inn, on your right is the church and beyond it the castle gates.

Hever

Hever Castle is a fortified manor-house. It was bought by Sir Geoffrey Bullen, a Norfolk man who made money in the City and was Lord Mayor, in the mid-fifteenth century. His son married into the minor aristocracy, his grandson made a match with a daughter of the Duke of Norfolk. This social-climbing Sir Thomas Bullen lies buried in the church, created an earl at last and father of a queen. He died in 1538, two years after his dreams crashed with the hideous death of the luckless Anne. His home Hever Castle, where Henry VIII courted first Anne's elder sister Mary, then Anne herself, was bought in a semi-ruinous condition by the first Lord Astor and restored between 1903 and 1906.

Markbeech
Returning down the lane past the *Henry VIII* inn, turn left at the end to go to Markbeech, keeping its church on your right and turning sharp right at the following T-junction, Horseshoe Green. This lane passes under the railway at Cowden station and up to the B2026 road. Across this a lane leads to Cowden village,

Cowden
another former Wealden iron-smelting centre with a shingle-spired church, like Hever's. Keep left past its church, cross the Kent Water at the bottom of the hill and climb up through Holtye Common, forking left to reach the A264 road. Follow this left until you reach the cross-roads with the B2026, and turn right on this to

Hartfield
Hartfield, a pretty village with plenty of inns.

For the next 6 miles you are in a part of the Weald which separates the area accessible from London from true rural seclusion (that is, it did before the age of railway and motor car). There are markedly fewer mansions built by Lord Mayors of London on the far side of Ashdown Forest. There is first, out from Hartfield, true forest with thick greenwood, then as the road climbs, bare windswept heights covered with gorse, bracken, and heather and occasional lone pines. Great vistas open up all round of distant purple hills, and wild, open, free country.

Your B2026 road at last meets the A22 and you turn left through Maresfield on the way to

Uckfield
Uckfield. This is a large market town with a High Street sloping down to the valley of a stream (utilised by the railway). It is full of shops, banks, and estate agencies, and there is a big old inn called the *Maiden's Head*.

When main roads in England were improved by their Turnpike Trusts, which imposed tolls for use by travellers, communication was easier and traffic increased. A glance at some of the buildings in Uckfield's High Street, many from the late eighteenth century, shows that business increased along with the traffic, to be augmented still further, as at Tunbridge Wells, when the railway arrived. Many a town and village moved away from its original nucleus, church and manor-house, to where the trade could be picked up.

Turning left immediately after passing over the railway at Uckfield, the B2102 road will take you through some delightful country with diversity in its woodlands and pastures, fine houses and hamlets, and still the Weald's protective screen of foliage to give the impression of rural remoteness, to Mayfield, to reach which turn left at Cross-in-Hand and take the A267.

Mayfield   Mayfield's long street, on the main A267 road, is lined on both sides with cottages and houses of great interest, especially perhaps *Middle House*, an inn dated 1575, in decorative black-and-white timber work such as you find in the West Midlands.

St Dunstan, Archbishop of Canterbury in the late tenth century, is alleged to have built the first palace and the first church in Mayfield, in wood as was the usual early English custom. The present church, in stone, came about five hundred years later, high, wide, and airy, with octagonal pillars. A local iron-master, Thomas Sands, lies buried under an iron slab, and you might notice that some of the letters and figures (N and 7, for example) are the wrong way round.

The story goes that it was St Dunstan who was responsible for the chalybeate spring at Tunbridge Wells. He was an expert goldsmith, and one day when he was practising his craft in his residence here (whether wooden palace or hermitic cell is debated) at Mayfield, the Devil appeared before him. Not being one for giving the enemy the least chance, St Dunstan instantly seized the Devil's nose with his red-hot tongs. The dark one jerked back, struggled free, ran howling to a certain spring south of Tonbridge, and plunged his nose in it to cool off. And that is why the spring became chalybeate and gave solace to so many malfunctioning livers.

Where the A267 sweeps left around the school buildings, carry straight on down Fletching Street past the celebrated *Carpenters Arms* (or not past it, according to choice) and follow the lane to Wadhurst. The way is precipitous, ascending and descending through dark woods, but you might notice an occasional name from the Weald's Iron Age: Cinder Hill, Forge Farm, like ghosts from a forgotten age. Turn right along the B2100 into Wadhurst, which grew with the railway, and continue along this road to Lamberhurst. The luxurious mansions behind banks of rhododendrons are also a product of railway propinquity.

Wadhurst

Lamberhurst

Lamberhurst, on the little River Teise, has several of the Weald's weatherboarded or tile-hung cottages, and also, in the river valley, it has Scotney Castle, the last of the tour's former great houses (for we are back within a few miles of Tunbridge Wells). Go a short way along the A21 main road to Hastings, and turn into a drive on the left, well signposted. At the end of the narrow drive is a spacious car park and the gate to the beautiful gardens.

Scotney Castle

The Hussey family, who created this landscaped Elysium, live in a stone Victorian house nearby at the top of the hill; at the bottom, in a lake made by a channel from the Teise, is a little round tower from the fourteenth century, and the ruins of a Tudor manor-house attached to it. All around this moated mystery, sloping gently down to it, are lawns, banks of rhododendrons, masses of flowers, great stately oaks, beeches, ashes, horse chestnuts, cedars, and pines. There are gravelled walks, wooden seats, the sound of the running water-courses underlying the mellifluous omnipresent birdsong, and all the sweet and fragrant intoxicating scents. The little castle itself, reflected in the dappled, silent water, its warm creamy-brown stone emanating faint echoes of past loves, laughter, tears, tragedies, radiates the essential magic of this enchanted garden.

Returning, if we must, to the pragmatic world and to Tunbridge Wells, you may take either the A21 through Lamberhurst, or the B2169 through Bells Yew Green: the two roads arrive at opposite ends of the town.

Maidstone

Tourist Information Office
Gatehouse, Old Palace Gardens, tel 673581

Population 70,920

Theatre
Hazlitt Theatre, Earl Street

Cinema
Granada, Lower Stone Street

Museums
Maidstone Museum and Art Gallery, St Faith's Street
Tyrwhitt-Drake Museum of Carriages, Archbishop's Stables

Places of Interest

Archbishop's Palace	The Master's House
Archbishop's Stables	Town Hall
All Saints Church	

Maidstone is the county town of Kent, its administrative headquarters, and has long been so. Canterbury might be the Church's capital, Rochester, Chatham and Dover centres for defence, Tunbridge Wells for fashion, and Ashford for industry, but since the very earliest days of Kent's existence as a shire rather than a small kingdom, Maidstone has been the centre for all legal transactions. Not that these generally took place within the town: to the north, now a suburban residential area, is Penenden Heath, and it was here that important cases were heard and decided, out in the open air. For example, there was the celebrated action between Archbishop Lanfranc and Bishop Odo of Bayeux, William the Conqueror's half-brother, who had presumptuously seized much of the archbishop's land in Kent; after three days, Lanfranc won it back.

There is a good car park on the roof of a huge new shopping complex called the Stoneborough Centre, accessible from King Street. The Centre is on several floors, and boasts all kinds of shops and a café, and is of course all indoors. If you emerge from it on the opposite side, in Romney Place, you can then follow Lower Stone Street downhill, with the cinema on your right, and turn left into Palace Avenue past the police station, and the bus station. At the end, where several streets meet, on your left is a huge barn-like structure of stone, with a timbered, brick-filled porch. This is the Archbishop's Stables, and houses the Tyrwhitt-Drake Museum of Carriages. Opposite, across the road, is the Archbishop's Palace, but it is better to proceed farther up College Road to the first of the group of ragstone buildings of the fourteenth century which distinguish the riverside of Maidstone. Of the first group, built as a college for secular canons by Archbishop Courtenay to serve the great parish church of All Saints and others in the area, there remain a small gateway, a tower, a large hall with towers, and a crenellated gatehouse which leads to the church and a tree-shaded walk by the river.

The church is wide and high, with a timbered roof and some rather alarming embellishments in the shape of wall-paintings and a reredos, added in 1910. The third in this group is the Archbishop's Palace, which predates the others; Archbishop Islip finished it in the 1350s, although much of the upper storey was rebuilt in the reign of Henry VIII in the early sixteenth century. All these buildings stand by the River Medway, which here at Maidstone is wide and handsome.

Through one of these gardens the little River Len flows before joining the Medway. Across this you can walk up Mill Street to the High Street, turning right and going up it, past the eighteenth-century clock of the Town Hall. Just past the *Royal Star Hotel* on your left you can turn into a passage to Market Buildings, where the old Corn Exchange, girt with little shops, has been turned into a professional theatre. Out in Earl Street you can turn almost immediately from it to St Faith's Street, where Chillington House, a large Elizabethan building with extensions in roughly the same style, houses the Public Library, the Adult Education Centre, and the Museum and Art Gallery.

St Faith's Street opens into Week Street, the lower end now reserved for pedestrians and full of shops at its junction with the High Street and King Street, and this is back in the middle of things. Across the way is the King Street entrance to the great Stoneborough Centre and its airy car park, from which you can see most of the town.

There is another sense in which Maidstone is the centre of Kent. There is a traditional separation within the county of Men of Kent from Kentish Men. The origins of the distinction are disputed, but I believe that basically it is possible that the Men of Kent, (those born east of the Medway) represent those very early settlers who established their Kingdom of Kent in the fifth or sixth century, and their descendants, and the Kentish Men are those who came into the county from London and elsewhere, since they are from west of the Medway. It is a very ancient nicety which is imperfectly understood within the county and not at all outside it.

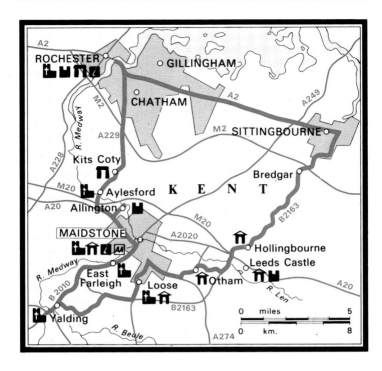

Maidstone – East Farleigh – Yalding – Loose – Otham – Leeds Castle – Hollingbourne – Rochester – Aylesford – Allington Castle – Maidstone

Tour length 64 miles

It should not be surprising, starting as we do in Maidstone, that this tour is concerned very much with the River Medway, its tributaries and its defences. A river, so vital to any stretch of country for life-giving water and for ease of communication within and overseas, also presents the problem of vulnerability, since that access so available to residents is just as available to invaders. These northern hills, the North Downs and the southern Chart Hills, breached by the river, are the most ancient seats of habitation, occupied thousands of years earlier than the forest depths of the Weald. You will see proof of that in the course of the tour. You will see also some of the reasons, in its fertile acres, for the fabled wealth of the Kentish farmers.

College Road, which has to be approached in the course of the one-way system which operates in Maidstone as in most towns apparently to confuse all strangers, leads to the B2010 through **Tovil** Tovil, where the old Royal Paper Mill stands, **East Farleigh** and runs along the riverside. Pause at East Farleigh and investigate the lane that goes down between the *Bull Inn* and the churchyard. It leads to the river, spanned here by a fourteenth-century stone bridge with pointed arches and ribbed vaulting. Here is the river in its green rural valley, quiet and placid with pleasure-boats moored, and the products of intense agriculture crowding both banks to the ridges above.

Beyond West Farleigh the road leaves the vivid valley and climbs the hill. All the way, through the hills to Maidstone, the river has flowed between two high banks; upstream in the plain, it meanders in many streams and is joined by many tributaries. One of them arrives as you sweep down the hill into the pretty street of **Yalding** Yalding, lined with brick, timbered, and tile-hung cottages of many differing periods. A very narrow bridge crosses the River Beult; follow the road another half mile and you will see a much larger bridge and the junction of another tributary, the Teise, with the Medway. There is a weir, an inn, and usually a good deal of aquatic activity.

Returning across the Yalding bridge, which was built in the fifteenth century, with the church's little Tudor onion spire on your right, go back up the street's hill and turn right on the winding lane to Hunton and Coxheath. It re-enters the hills, but if you turn right on the B2163, then left on the main A229 road towards Maidstone, you can, by taking a turning off the main road to the Loose   left dip into the by-passed village of Loose.

There have been many guesses at the origin of the name Loose, some claiming that it comes from the stream that runs through it, because it goes underground here and there, and 'loses' itself, and there have been jokes about the Loose Women's Institute and all other variations of the same pun, but the name appears to derive, prosaically enough, from a synonym for a pigsty. Pigsty or not, Loose is beautiful. The little splashing stream seems to be everywhere, running before and behind the old cottages, all on a steep bank about the church. One house, taller and longer than the rest, is a Wool House from the fifteenth century, timber-framed, in-filled with lath and plaster, and once used as a workshop for weavers. All about is the sound of water, reminiscent of some quiet mountain village in the Swiss Alps.

The Swiss Alps, however, do not have to contend with the proximity of the constant growl of traffic on the A229. Leave the village, turning towards Maidstone, and when after a mile you come to the junction with the A274, turn right on it. All about are housing estates, but at the end of them there is a lane turning left to Otham which spirits you away at once from these Maidstone suburbs and back into the dark-wooded by-ways Otham   of the hills. Quarries near Otham provided the grey stone known as Kentish Rag, that built many of the county's palaces, castles, and churches and ensured the affluence of Otham quarrymen. The house of one of them, significantly called Stoneacre, is an excellent example of such a good small house; part stone, part timber, it lies deep in the close-forested green valley below Otham's street, and is open on Wednesday and Saturday afternoons in the summer season.

Leeds Castle is the next objective, and there are two ways of getting there. One is easy, you simply follow the lane from Otham down to the main A2020 road, turn right on it, and right again past the *Great Danes Hotel*. The other is much more complicated, difficult, and interesting. At the bottom of the hill from Otham there is a lane turning off right by the bridge over the little River Len. Follow this in its horrifically twisting course through the most bucolic of farmland, past very few houses (one of which, however, is a magnificent sixteenth-century timbered hall-house), until it emerges on the B2163 road whereon lies the village of Leeds. There are several good inns in the village, some more medieval timbered houses, the remains of a priory, and a church with a huge twelfth-century tower.

Leeds

Fully to enjoy Leeds Castle and its park you must have fine weather and be fit, because it is a very long way from the car park to the castle. The walk itself, provided the above-mentioned conditions are obtaining, is immensely rewarding, because full use has been made of the waters of the River Len. Lakes, ponds, and channels have been created in which all manner of wild-fowl have made their home: many species of duck, geese, and swans (including black swans), and in addition guinea fowl and peacocks. As there are black swans, one supposes white peacocks to have been indispensable. The trees in the park are old, tall, and splendid, but the castle itself, like a larger, completed, and habitable form of Scotney, is straight out of the pages of some fairy story, on an island in a lake formed centuries ago by damming the Len.

The ruins of a barbican of the late thirteenth century lie to the left of the present causeway, which leads to a gatehouse. Within the walls are a lawn and the keep building; a palace rather than a fortress, but visitors must skirt the walls and follow a path down by the lake, entering eventually by a curious subterranean passage lined with barrels. These cellars are the oldest part, their origins probably lying in Norman times.

The principal block, into which you emerge from the murky depths, was once a medieval fortress keep but was rebuilt in Henry VIII's time as palatial apartments and rendered habitable again in the last century. It is fully glazed and furnished and in excellent state, with furniture, tapestry, and ornaments from the sixteenth century, the time of its rebuilding. One of its rooms, hung with modern pictures and a couple of Impressionists, a Degas and a Pissarro, is filled with a board-room table and chairs: a clue to one of the castle's present functions, as a conference centre. There is a small internal courtyard with a fountain and a chapel, and the whole circuit of rooms can be visited before issuing into the lawned castle yard. Other attractions apart from the parkland itself include an aviary and a golf course.

Turn right from the castle drive to get to the A2020, and go straight across it, keeping to the B2163. Quite soon, just after the village sign-plate for Hollingbourne, there is a turning to the **Eyhorne Manor** left to Eyhorne Manor. This is a splendid example of an early fifteenth-century hall-house, the kind of timber-framed house still found all over Kent and Sussex, built in sufficiently large numbers in the late Middle Ages to indicate what wealth could be derived from the good land there, whether it was used to grow crops or to rear wool-bearing sheep.

The village at the end of its drive is in fact Eyhorne Street: one actually comes to **Hollingbourne** Hollingbourne after passing under the railway bridge and scaling the lower slopes of a steep hill. The village is delightful, with some very old, typically Kentish (tile-hung, weatherboarded, timber-framed) houses and cottages, and at the top, just before the road stands you on your ear to scramble up what seems to be the north face of the Eiger, a fine brick Tudor house which once belonged to a branch of the ubiquitous Kentish Culpepper family.

The mountain you have just crawled up, ice-axes at the ready, is not actually a section of the Alps but part of the North Downs, and you have climbed its south-facing scarp slope. On your B2163 road you now roll gently down the northern side, and on your way if you look to either side you may see more evidence of Kentish wealth: mile upon mile of orchards, apple and cherry for the most part. Spring is the best time of year for this district, the trees then pink and white with blossom. There are few villages, only Bredgar, after which you cross a bridge over the teeming M2 motorway, and Tunstall, and then **Sittingbourne** you are among the back streets of Sittingbourne. When you arrive at the junction with its High Street, turn left and drive through it, and keep driving in that direction, for you are on the old A2 which is the even older Watling Street, an English name given to the older still *via strata* of Roman Britain that led from Dover to London, then on across the province to the legionary fortress at Chester. For half the distance at this point it is, admittedly, dull, but follow it through Newington, Rainham, and the outskirts of Gillingham and Chatham until you slide down the great hill of the Downs and enter Rochester.

Rochester   There are car parks, but if all else fails there is usually room on the Esplanade, the road between the castle walls and the river. Rochester is worth exploration. Like Canterbury, it was a town in pre-Roman Celtic Britain, and had a bridge across the Medway. The Romans replaced it and built a military fort. Some of their building material can be seen in the medieval work of both castle and city walls. St Augustine in 604 made it the second episcopal see in England. The bishop of the late eleventh century, Gundulph, built both the first stone castle and the existing cathedral, whose lovely Romanesque west front and high rounded nave arches show the quality of his work. The great square Norman keep was added to the castle in the time of Henry I, in 1130. The Department of the Environment (because it was a royal castle, like Dover) has preserved it, made it safe for visitors, and inserted floors, stairs, and platforms, the better to view it. From its high turrets you can look out over a superb panoramic view of the town and the wide, winding Medway as it sweeps round past the old naval dockyard at Chatham and out to sea.

Rochester High Street is rich from end to end, from Chertsey's Gate into the cathedral precinct, past the four-square *Royal Victoria and Bull Hotel*, the Guildhall of 1687 with a ship weathervane, the Corn Exchange still projecting its clock over the street, some survivors of its medieval timbered houses, and finally, flanked on either side by stretches of the city walls, a late sixteenth-century brick house, Eastgate House. This is the home not only of the city's museum but also of a large collection of Charles Dickens's odds and ends, since he lived at Gadshill on the far side of the river and based some of his novels' action on Rochester. In the garden of Eastgate stands the little painted Swiss chalet in which he used to work, transferred from Gadshill's garden.

At the top of Star Hill, where you entered Rochester on the A2, a fork right (now ascending the hill) is the A229 which will take you out of this Medway conurbation, over the Downs past Rochester's little airfield, and down Bluebell Hill on the scarp slope again. At the bottom of the hill a sign points left to Aylesford. The lane turns round and dives under the A229, and almost at once you are confronted by two possible directions, a sign pointing to Kits Coty House, and apparently nowhere to park. It is nevertheless worth looking for some suitable corner to leave the car, because the path that leads back up the slope brings you to the fore-mentioned visible evidence of habitation hereabouts some 4,000 years ago. The two huge stones, with a massive **Kits Coty** capstone across the top, known as Kits Coty **House** House constitute the entrance to a Neolithic burial chamber, the main part of which has disappeared. Lower down the hill lie the scattered remnants of another such chamber, called Little Kits Coty, or the Countless Stones, since no one has ever made them the same number twice running.

The lane the Kits Coty path leads from goes on **Aylesford** to Aylesford, set steeply on the right bank of the river, its church at the top. Its streets are very narrow, and its bridge, being old and narrower still, has been rendered one-way, and a new one built for you to cross. There is room for you to park, if there is time, to look at the village and enjoy its heaped-up antiquities, which include at its down-river end a medieval friary reoccupied since 1949 by Carmelite friars, whose predecessors established themselves there in 1237.

The Carmelites have also performed wonders with Allington Castle. Having crossed the river, fork left and go straight up to the A20 road, turning left and following it for about a mile, through British Legion Village. Then take the turning left to Allington Castle, which is at the end of the lane, by the river. If you are lucky, you might just catch the last guided tour (at 3.45pm). The castle was built in the thirteenth century by Sir Stephen de Penchester (the Lord Warden who built a manor-house at Penshurst) as a defence for Maidstone. In the 1490s it was bought and made habitable, with a cottage in the inner courtyard, by one Sir Henry Wyatt, a man lucky enough to have survived a spell in the Tower of London under Richard III (kept supplied, so the story goes, by an obliging cat). His son Sir Thomas, a poet of distinction, lived there, and so did his grandson, another Sir Thomas, until he raised a rebellion against Queen Mary I's proposed marriage with the Catholic King of Spain in 1554. He lost the rebellion, his castle, and his head. By the nineteenth century the castle was partly ruinous, and partly roofed as a farmhouse. In an appallingly run-down condition it was bought early this century by Lord Conway, who spent vast sums on making it good again. Subsequently it was given to the Carmelites, who tend it and use it as a retreat and keep the flock of brown pigeons, which are the descendants of some brought from Italy by the poet Sir Thomas. There is necessarily much replica building, but it is so well done that it does not detract from the fact that you are, substantially, in another genuine inhabited medieval castle.

From Allington you have only two miles to go back to Maidstone.

Allington Castle (margin note)

Sevenoaks

Tourist Information Centre
Caravan in Buckhurst Lane

Population 18,100

Cinema
Focus, South Park

Places of Interest
Knole
Parish Church
Sevenoaks School

The above information, thinly spread as it is, may give the impression that Sevenoaks has few attractions. On its hill at the southern end of the Darent valley, it is an old market town with plenty of shops, inns, hotels, and other amenities, and its share of houses surviving from earlier times. Moreover it has two important qualifications as one of the centres for this book: first, it is an excellent base from which to explore this highly interesting area, and second, the great palace of Knole is on its doorstep.

Sevenoaks School was founded by one William Sevenoak or Sennocke, named after the town because he was an orphan, who was apprenticed to a grocer in London, made money in the city, and served as Lord Mayor immediately before the famous Whittington. When he died in 1432 he left money for a grammar school in his home town where poor children could be taught free.

In the church is the tomb of William Lambarde, the Elizabethan writer, who tells Sennocke's story in his *Perambulation of Kent.* A short way past the church on the other side of the street is the drive into Knole Park. The oaks and beeches are old, stately, and dignified, and between them you may see some of the large herd of deer which inhabits the Park. Beyond the trees, on the knoll which gives the place its name, is the most magnificent Jacobean mansion in southern England.

It was begun in the 1470s as an archbishop's palace, acquired by the covetous Henry VIII, and given by his daughter Elizabeth to her Lord Treasurer Lord Buckhurst, formerly Sir Thomas Sackville. The present long front and square gatehouse are his work. His descendants, as Earls of Dorset in the seventeenth century, Dukes of Dorset in the eighteenth, and Barons Sackville to the present day, have lived in it ever since.

The house is consequently filled with this family's accumulated goods, furniture, ornaments, silver, portraits, memories, and possibly also ghosts, in unusual continuity. Stories abound: of Lady Betty Germaine who had a suite of rooms in the house and lived her life in them; of the 3rd Duke who went to Italy to collect classical treasures and brought back another kind, the beautiful Giannetta Baccelli, whose stone likeness reclines at the foot of the staircase; of the tragic death of the 4th Duke; of the Countess of Desmond, who lived for 140 years, was said to have danced with Richard III, and died in James I's time. The house needs to be visited slowly, to have its stories explained, its atmosphere absorbed, savoured, and appreciated. Then its unique qualities will linger in your memory, and you will be the richer for them.

Westerham

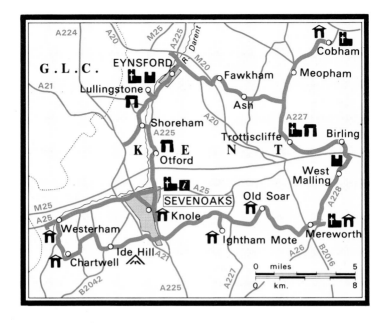

Sevenoaks – Shoreham – Lullingstone – Eynsford – Meopham – Cobham – Trottiscliffe – West Malling – Mereworth – Ightham – Ide Hill – Chartwell – Westerham – Sevenoaks

Tour length 68 miles

The little River Darent cuts its way through the great chalk North Downs, and constitutes the first truly rural area in Kent going eastward from London. Consequently it is remarkably rich in the kind of house likely to be built by opulent London merchants, courtiers, or politicians, who need to be within reach of the City, Court, or Commons. The high ridge of the Chart Hills to its south, on which Sevenoaks stands, commands views over central Kent which, on a clear day, might rival any in the background of an Italian Renaissance painting, and therefore has attracted, over the long years, many of these country-house retreats.

Setting forth down the High Street of Sevenoaks, northward past the ancient and famous Sevenoaks Vine cricket ground, you emerge at a cross-roads by the *Bat and Ball* tavern. Go straight ahead on the A225 road towards Dartford, following the Darent along its deep and lovely valley in the Downs. You come first to Otford, where there is a duckpond, and nearby the ruins of an early sixteenth-century palace for the archbishops of Canterbury. At just over a mile from where the road at Otford swings round left after the railway station, take a turning left under a railway bridge to the delightful village of Shoreham, through which the Darent splashes its shallow, clear way beneath the bridges. The artist Samuel Palmer lived and painted here, as might anyone with pleasure in so pretty a place in so verdant a valley. At the top of the village street turn right, and keep branching right as the lane traverses the valley and brings you back to the A225 very close to the lane leading to Lullingstone.

Apart from Lullingstone Castle, which is actually a privately owned brick Tudor mansion with a little church, there is the very well preserved and presented Roman villa here at Lullingstone, as substantial a palace as any of its kind, with some fine mosaics and evidence in wall-paintings that at one period (after 380) one of its rooms was in use as a Christian chapel.

Eynsford From Lullingstone, back on the A225 valley road, it is not far to Eynsford, which has an aged bridge beside a ford across the Darent, some timbered and weatherboarded cottages, a fine old steepled church, and, a little farther upstream, the crumbled stone walls of a small Norman castle, re-fortified in about 1100. At the Farningham cross-roads it would be desirable to turn right, but this is prohibited, so one must go left to the first roundabout and return to the spot the other way. The road is the A20, and it is permitted to turn off it first left, by a lane that leads to the entrance gates of the Brands Hatch motor-racing circuit. The lane is also crossed at this point by the modern M20 motorway, and the best thing to do is to pass under it down to Fawkham Green, turn right at the end, go up a narrow lane signposted to Ash, and turn left at

Ash the top. In Ash you pass the lane to the church and turn left by an inn, making for Ridley and Meopham. There is a maze of lanes hereabouts and some of the kind of scenery to be found all along the North Downs, deeply scored with sudden long valleys, heavily wooded on the tops and cultivated with orchards and arable fields in the bottoms. Villages are small and pretty, and if you keep travelling eastward you should arrive at the A227. Turn left on this in the direction of

Meopham Gravesend and you will soon come to Meopham, where there is a large village green, an inn called the *Cricketers* (indicating the usual activities on the green), and a windmill. Go through it past the church and turn right on the B2009 road to

Cobham Cobham. It is not far: as the road turns sharply right to the village there is opposite a small but fine late seventeenth-century brick house called Owletts which can be visited on Wednesday and Thursday afternoons.

Cobham is justly famous for its aged inn, the *Leather Bottle*, which of course proclaims its use by Dickens for a story in his *Pickwick Papers*, and its group of almshouses by the church, formerly a college of priests for the service of neighbouring parishes. In the chancel of the church, around the elaborate family tomb of the Brokes, there are fifteen large brasses, showing earlier members of the family on their tomb-stones, some of the best examples of this kind of memorial in England.

Even Theseus needed Ariadne's help to get out of the Labyrinth, and I will not attempt to guide you through the lanes between Cobham and Trottiscliffe: the scenery is superb, but even that might pall after you have seen it, going round in circles, for the twenty-seventh time. The alternative is to return along the B2009, go back along the A227 through Meopham and on south-ward to the edge of the North Downs' scarp slope. Watch out for an inn on the left called the *Vigo*: a lane leads off beside it and plunges very steeply down the scarp. Avoid it in wet weather because it turns into a rushing torrent, but it takes you, with a gravity-resistant wriggle at the

Trottiscliffe bottom, down to Trottiscliffe. It is worth taking the lane, left in the village, to the church, and then the footpath from it to find the Coldrum Stones, which constitute another Neolithic burial chamber like Kits Coty. In this case, the stones are in position around a mound, but the uprights are without a capstone. A number of skeletons were found within the mound in years past, and some bones are preserved in the church.

Instead of going straight from Trottiscliffe to the A20, take the left turning and travel through the farmland at the foot of the tree-lined Downs to the villages Ryarsh and Birling. Turn right by

Birling Birling church, then left after crossing over the M20 motorway to reach the A228. Turn right on

Leybourne this, and there on the right close to Leybourne church you can see the drum towers of the fortified gatehouse to its manor-house, known as Leybourne Castle. The A228 soon meets the A20 and shortly goes off left to West Malling.

West Malling The wide High Street of West Malling is full of exceptionally good-looking houses, many from the days of the Stuarts and the early Georges.

There is an abbey at West Malling, built by the industrious Bishop Gundulph of Rochester, and there is a little protective tower, accessible from the A228 at the top end of the town, by the lane to Offham. After West Malling the road passes through the fringe of Mereworth Woods and runs gradually down to Mereworth. If you turn left on the A26 for $\frac{1}{2}$ mile and stop outside an impressive set of gates, you can catch a glimpse through them of the astonishing outline of Mereworth Castle, which is as far from being a castle as Lullingstone. It was built in the eighteenth century by the Earl of Westmorland, replacing the existing manor-house, on the highly fashionable lines of Palladio's Villa Capra at Vicenza. Fully on the squared circle principle, this rotunda is one of only two surviving examples in England (the other is Chiswick House) of this exotic style.

If you now return to Mereworth, cross over the A228, keeping the tall and unusual spire of Mereworth church (also built by the earl to replace the existing church, inconveniently sited near his Italian extravaganza) on your left, cross over the B2016 road, skirt West Peckham, keep right along the fringes of Mereworth Woods, and then follow a sign left to Old Soar Manor, you will have tracked down a remarkable survival.

Medieval manor-houses, the domestic quarters of a feudal tenant, have in the natural run of things mainly been replaced by more comfortable or fashionable or modern dwellings, and there are therefore very few left standing. In this very out-of-the-way spot, as you will appreciate from the difficulty in finding it, on the warm southern slopes of the Chart Hills, there stands a fragment of one, which you may enter and explore, since it is open nearly all the time. The great hall was long ago demolished and replaced by an eighteenth-century house, but the lord's solar, with storeroom beneath, remains, and what you see in excellent condition has stood for some 700 years.

Follow the lane from Old Soar to Plaxtol, then turn right on the A227 and quickly left off it; at Ivy Hatch turn sharp left down a narrow, thickly wooded lane to Ightham Mote, also on the southern slopes of these hills. It is not always possible to see inside this wonderful moated manor-house, since it is open only on Friday and Sunday afternoons, but you can view it quite happily from the path by the moat. This is a much larger foundation than Old Soar, moated and fortified and rebuilt, with a stout gatehouse, in the sixteenth century, on four sides of a square with a courtyard in the middle. Set in idyllic gardens in a remote Arcadian valley, it could capture the affection and imagination of anyone fortunate enough to be connected with it. As at Scotney, a subtle enchantment in its atmosphere, in the sweetly scented air, in the sun-warmed lichen-encrusted walls, or the bright reflections in the moat, could captivate any susceptible visitor.

Ivy Hatch Return up the lane to Ivy Hatch (the *Plough Inn* on the corner, like most of the others you will have passed, offers warming sustenance to travellers) and take the left fork by the inn, heading for Bitchet Green and Fawke Common. The lane weaves through cool lofty woods, along the tops of the hills. You have to fork left again, cut across two cross-roads, and then skirt the southern wall (on your right) of Knole Park, turn right and drive up the hill on the A225 but almost at once turn off left. The lane wriggles, crosses over the A21, and dives into the woods again before emerging at the B2042 at Ide Hill.

Ide Hill From the war memorial park at Ide Hill, the day being bright and clear and visibility good, you may stand and wonder at the great wide patchwork carpet spread out below you. Ide Hill is one of the highest points of these hills, and southward all mid-Kent is at your feet, its greeny-blue texture dappled with here and there a flash of water, a jumble of russet roofs, the lighter shades of the crop-bearing fields, the white-vaned tips of clusters of oast-kilns.

Go north from Ide Hill on the lane that skirts the church, and after $\frac{1}{2}$ mile turn left, then left again, passing on your left an inn called the *Fox and Hounds*. Forking right at Toy's Hill (where again there is the same enormous vista of the Eden Valley and the hills beyond), and then turning right at a T-junction with another lane, winding back up into the woods you soon come to a high brick wall on the right and the entrance to the capacious car park of Chartwell.

Chartwell The house of Chartwell is a pleasant if unremarkable brick building with a high crow-stepped gable, the gardens are beautifully landscaped and tended, and the site, in a steep re-entrant of the south-facing hills, is as harmonious as any. But what brings visitors by the coach-load and by the thousand and necessitates both the car park and the wooden refreshment room, is that from 1924 until his death in 1965 Chartwell was the home of Mr (later Sir) Winston Churchill. Since there is little else in the house itself to attract attention, every room is filled with pictures of him and by him (for many of his paintings are on display), photographs, clothes, and memorabilia of all sorts. If you wish to pay homage to him as to any other great man, then to visit Chartwell is richly rewarding.

Westerham Another great man, whose career was over far too early, spent half his short life in Westerham, and two houses in it preserve for him what Chartwell does for Churchill. This is General James Wolfe, who by a combination of dogged perseverance, desperation, and ingenuity, fought the French out of Canada. To reach Westerham follow the lane uphill from Chartwell and turn right on the B2026 road. Wolfe's old home, a big square brick seventeenth-century block called Quebec House, faces you on the junction with the A25. Parking does not appear to be easy, but if you can find a space the house is open every afternoon except Thursday and Saturday.

The other house that carries on the Wolfe tradition is Squerryes Court, to reach which you go through Westerham (observing the statues of Churchill and Wolfe on either ends of the green) and take a lane on the left just outside the town. Squerryes is of slightly later date and more elegant style, in whose grounds, while visiting, Wolfe received his first commission in the army.

From Westerham it is a short distance back along the A25 to Sevenoaks.

Lewes

Tourist Information Office
187 High Street, tel 6151

Population 14,380

Museums
Barbican Museum, Barbican House
Anne of Cleves House Museum

Places of Interest
Castle
St Michael's Church
Priory ruins
Anne of Cleves House
Southover Grange
Fifteenth-Century Bookshop
Bull House

In the days when the sea was regarded solely from the practical viewpoint of a medium which could provide food and on which goods or persons could be transported, albeit with danger and difficulty, the huge sprawling conurbations of Brighton, Worthing, Eastbourne, and Bexhill existed as nothing but very small fishing villages. Defensible sites in the gaps in the Downs made by its rivers were far more important: Lewes was one of these, on a hill close by the River Ouse where it cuts through the South Downs on its way to the sea. Here a castle was built and a town developed alongside it.

Lewes therefore consists mainly of a High Street running up from the river to the top of the hill below the castle walls, and lateral streets leaving it at right angles, to the south very steeply to the river plain.

The castle gateway, the Barbican, is not used as its entrance, which is up a precipitous series of steps, reached through a gate and a small lawn. The Barbican was the last contribution of the occupying Warrenne family, in the fourteenth century, and is built mainly of flints. William de Warenne, a doughty supporter of William the Conqueror, had built the original castle, with two mounds instead of the usual one, and a keep on each. Part of one of them remains, but most of the structure was sold off as building material in the seventeenth century.

The Georgian house close by the Barbican is the centre of the Sussex Archaeological Society and houses its museum, which like the castle is open daily. Nearby is a little church with a round tower, St Michael's, which is thought to have been the castle's chapel.

In the High Street, just before the quick descent to the river, the big Georgian *White Hart Hotel* faces the classical portico of the Town Hall. The lanes running off the White Hart's side of the street throw themselves recklessly down to the adjoining hamlet Southover, and how their inhabitants manage in icy weather one cannot imagine. At the bottom of Keere Street there is a stone house built in 1572 called Southover Grange, the home of the diarist John Evelyn, with fine gardens attached. At right angles, and up a slight rise is Southover High Street. Close by its church of St John the Baptist a lane leads to the crumbled walls of the priory, which was one of the very few monasteries in England attached to the great Benedictine house of Cluny in France.

Farther along Southover High Street, past a pleasing Georgian terrace, on the right is the house given to the unfortunate Anne of Cleves to live in, after Henry VIII had decided that he could not tolerate such an unexciting wife. The house looks like a fifteenth-century hall-house, of timber and brick, flint and tile, and numerous later additions. It contains a museum and is open daily.

Keere Street ascends apparently perpendicularly (to the pedestrian) from Southover Grange to Lewes High Street, and contains many Georgian-fronted houses which are, it is claimed, much older behind their façades. On the corner at the top is one which remains undisguised and calls itself (to prove it) the Fifteenth Century Bookshop. On the same side in the High Street is another house of the same period, a tea-shop called Bull House; in it for a time limed the radical writer Tom Paine, an anti-monarchist and fervent supporter of revolutions, whether American or French.

There is plenty to interest the stroller around Lewes, for it is a town of character and antiquity, and from it roads lead out in all directions for the exploration of the Sussex Downs.

Lewes – Brighton – Newhaven – Glynde – Alfriston – Beachy Head – Eastbourne – Pevensey – Herstmonceux – Hailsham – Michelham Priory – Lewes

Tour length 80 miles

The South Downs, like the North Downs, are chalk hills, which run in a range from Salisbury Plain along the south coast and terminate in a series of high white cliffs, the last of which is Beachy Head. They differ in character from the North Downs in that they are generally less afforested, and stand out more dramatically between the inland country and the sea. There is no gently declining northern slope, but steep hills on both sides, and they have often been compared with a whale's back. The tour will explore one of their valleys, some of their seaside towns, one of their cliffs, and some of the inland country.

Brighton

The A27 main road cuts baldly through the hills from Lewes to Brighton, like the railway which keeps it company. Brighton is worth visiting, because it is the most senior and certainly the most exotic of the south coast towns developed deliberately for the benefit of holiday visitors. Its importance and reputation were fostered by the attention of George, Prince of Wales, eldest son of and for some years Regent for George III. It is from his time (late eighteenth, early nineteenth century) that many of the architecturally most pleasing buildings originate. There is also a large multi-storey car park, which offers neither aesthetic nor historical pleasure but is very useful, since it is central, and from it you can walk quickly down to the sea-front.

Between the two piers are some of the great hotels: the classical gull-white Belle Epoque elegance of the *Grand* contrasts with the terracotta Byzantine magnificence of the *Metropole*, and the establishments filling the slightly decayed grandeur of Regency Square, like a down-at-heel dowager duchess. Hotels proliferate like pebbles on the beach, but it is the complex area called the Lanes which offers most attraction.

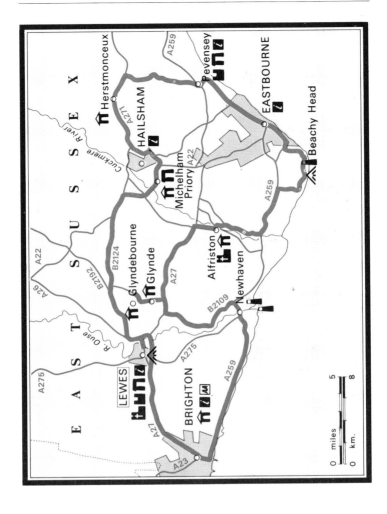

This is the older part of Brighton, a maze of narrow streets and alleys, like sterilised English souks, full of antique shops, boutiques, junk shops (peddling old and new junk), coffee-bars, inns, little piazzas with rain-defiant tables and chairs, and a good deal of both natural and synthetic charm. Parts have been rebuilt in a commendably sympathetic style, striving to retain the essentially 'quaint' character, a contrast to Regency formality.

Find your way through, if you can, eastward, to where the Royal Pavilion rears its improbable minarets and domes above the homely Sussex trees and pigeons. This was a straightforward eighteenth-century house capriciously transmogrified by order of the Prince of Wales into something out of the Arabian Nights. Currently in pale green and buff, this oriental extravaganza is open most of the time, outdoing Aladdin's cave, and is flanked by another stately pleasure-dome, decreed by the same princely Kublai Khan, in similar architectural vein: at least this latter has been useful as a theatre and concert hall.

The A259 road, which runs along half the south coast of England, is the promenade road at Brighton. If you follow it eastward, past the Palace Pier, the forbidding blocks of the girls' school, Roedean, on the wind-blown hillside overlooking the sea, and St Dunstan's Hospital, it will take you over the hills, through the unexciting streets of Peacehaven, down to **Newhaven** Newhaven, a bustling, busy harbour at the River Ouse's mouth. On the far side of the harbour, turn off left on the B2109 road, an extension of the A27, along the eastern side of the Ouse valley. When it joins the A27, turn right, and **Glynde** then first left to Glynde.

Glynde Place, in its east-facing grounds above the village, is a fine stone Tudor mansion with some excellent paintings (some Lelys, Zoffanys and Rubens cartoons), open to the public on Wednesday and Thursday afternoons during the summer. If you continue along the lane, deeper into a lovely green valley screened by hill-top woods, you will see on your right the phenomenon of Glyndebourne.

Glyndebourne   A pleasant but otherwise undistinguished mock-Jacobean brick house in this undisturbed Sussex vale a mile or two from Lewes has achieved international repute by being turned into a small but élite opera-house. The high scenery-loft is just visible behind the house, and through the stable archways much movement and activity are astir; perhaps cars draw up in the gravelled courtyard, maybe a helicopter waits in the adjoining paddock. The serene Sussex hills enclose artistic achievements with which Covent Garden, Place de l'Opéra, the Opernring, and La Scala have more in common.

Returning to the A27 and turning left, continue along it until you come to a signpost pointing Alfriston   right to Alfriston, which is in the valley of the Cuckmere river, a much smaller stream which nevertheless once had sufficient power to carve its passage through the mighty chalk Downs. Alfriston has a free car park, because it is something of a show-place, with all the attendant tea-shops, gift-shops, and antique shops suitable to such celebrity. It has some venerable and picturesque houses, the chief of which is the *Star Inn*, which is reckoned to be in part the thirteenth-century hostel built by the Abbot of Battle and much resorted to for sanctuary by thieves and fugitives. Across the road is the timbered and also genuinely antique inn the *George*, and if you take a footpath from the High Street down to the spacious green above which stands the steepled church, you can see to its right the Clergy House. An early hall-house, of the fourteenth century, timber-framed and lath-and-plaster in-filled, and thatched as it probably was when built, it is kept in excellent condition. It holds the distinction of being the first building to be purchased by the National Trust (for £10 in 1896). It is open to visitors on most days.

The fine inns of Alfriston may be augmented by Litlington   one in Litlington, across the Cuckmere and right (with caution because the lane is as much used as it is narrow), and if this lane is followed all along the east side of the narrow valley, whose houses are mainly of flint and whose sides are more thickly forested than in other downland valleys, it brings you again to the A259 coast road. Turn left on this as it climbs steeply from the Cuckmere estuary to the cliff-top, with the sea on your right, then plunges through Friston to a **Eastdean** bottom at Eastdean. Take here a turning right through another narrow defile called Birling Gap; a quiet green dip runs behind the sea-cliffs, carrying the road and usually a number of people who choose this unspoilt vale for a family picnic. Eastward the road climbs frenetically to what seems an immense height and levels out to a windy plain, most of which is a car park, with a convenient inn, and a stretch of chalky grass and gorse separating you from the sheer cliff called Beachy Head.

At the cliff's foot a lighthouse, diminished to a toy by the awful height, is washed by the sapphire sea. Gulls scream above and below about the cliff-face and the world about you is cold, immense, and frightening. At the top of a bare mountain, in a small boat far out at sea, or alone in a pathless and shelterless moor you may feel it acutely: here you can merely shiver, then turn away from the chasm and go back to the car park.

The road takes you down from the heights, the **Eastbourne** easternmost Downs, through Eastbourne, a highly respectable watering-place which took advantage of Brighton's success and followed suit: all the resorts blossomed once connected with London by the railway, which brought visitors cheaply by the thousand. The A259 takes you away from Eastbourne towards a beach called the Crumbles, then swings inland to cross the levels, marshy and watery like Romney Marsh, to Pevensey.

Pevensey In September 1066 these marshy levels were mud-flats, covered at high tide, and it was on a shore-line which began at Pevensey that Duke William and his Normans beached and clambered out to begin their headstrong venture. The promontory of Pevensey was already fortified (although ungarrisoned), the walls of the Roman Saxon Shore fort of Anderida stood then as they do now: and they had stood for over 700 years then. Unusually for a Roman fort, but probably following the contours of the promontory, the enclosed space was not a rectangle but elliptical.

The construction is familiar, based on alternating courses of stone and brick, thick and massive, with great solid bastions at intervals. Within the fort the Normans, their conquest complete, built a castle, moated with a curtain wall and a keep. Strengthened at intervals, it was an important stronghold throughout the Middle Ages, but now it is in poor repair, the keep gone, and only the towers added in the thirteenth century remaining, with parts of the wall. There is also a gruesome reminder of medieval methods in a hole-in-the-ground dungeon called an *oubliette*, for the logical reason that prisoners could conveniently be forgotten in it.

The castle is open most of the time, and there are also in Pevensey the Mint House, an antique shop which charges admittance to see its medieval interior, and the Customs House Museum: Pevensey became a limb of the Cinque Port Hastings.

A little way out of the village on the A259 towards Hastings there is a turning left which carries you pleasantly across the levels with the customary twists, turns, willows, sluices, and **Wartling** sheep, peculiar to marsh roads, to Wartling on the edge of firm land, then inland to the Royal Greenwich Observatory based on the castle and **Herstmonceux** parkland of Herstmonceux. At its entrance a notice proclaims that the telescope of Sir Isaac Newton is on show, and possibly within the grounds you may catch a glimpse of the rose-red brick castle, almost a Gothic Revival of the fifteenth century.

Herstmonceux stands on the A271 road, which your lane joins. Turn left on it through the village and go to Hailsham, a busy little market centre. Although unexceptional as an English country town, Hailsham is rare in one respect: its topography and inhabitants are marvellously well chronicled in one era, the late nineteenth century, by one Thomas Geering, a townsman. Find his *Our Sussex Parish* and you will learn much of the look and feel of country life a hundred years ago: it was published in 1884.

Follow the A295 through the town until it meets the A22, and cross this on a lane signposted to **Michelham** Michelham Priory. It is not long before the towered gatehouse of this foundation comes into sight on the right, and there are large car parks. In a loop of the Cuckmere river 'we have the old dwelling of the fat Abbots of Michelham', as Geering puts it. What exists is a remnant (the gatehouse and the refectory wing) of an Augustinian priory, the rest of which was demolished at the Dissolution in the sixteenth century and a house built, no doubt from the same material, by the purchasing family Pelham. There is a mill and a barn and sundry outbuildings, and the whole moated estate is now fully exploited by the Sussex Archaeological Trust, which owns it. It is open daily and offers a variety of exhibitions, events, entertainments of a rural nature, and sundry other attractions in its serene, sequestered setting. The inevitable corollary of such hectic activity, unfortunately, is that much of the former serenity, along with the enchantment of the place, is lost.

Upper Dicker The lane past the Priory emerges at Upper Dicker, and directly opposite on the road is another lane leading to Lower Dicker on the A22. This, the B2124 joining the B2192, and finally the A26 will take you back to Lewes.

Chichester

Tourist Information Office
The Council House, North Street, tel 82226

Population 20,940

Theatre
Chichester Festival Theatre

Places of Interest
Cathedral   St Mary's Hospital
Market Cross   Roman walls
Guildhall

Not many cities planned and laid out in Roman times have retained their street plan, but a citizen of *Noviomagus Regnensium* would not only find that large sections of the city walls remain in Chichester, but that if he came in by West Gate, he would not have too much difficulty in finding his way out by North Gate. The basic cross-pattern remains, even if nothing much else above ground does. That being the case, it is easy to find one's way around the blocks made by North, East, South and West Streets without getting lost.

The middle of the town is a pedestrian area, and the absence of traffic has encouraged a pavement-café experiment, never easy in our climate, enhanced by the early sixteenth-century Market Cross bang in the centre of the cross-roads. In all the streets there are many late medieval, sixteenth, seventeenth, and eighteenth-century houses, and as usual it is the ecclesiastical buildings which are the oldest, such as the thirteenth-century St Mary's Hospital off St Martin's Street, (the North-East block) and of course the Cathedral (the South-West block).

The Cathedral is basically Norman, with a fine three-storey nave, but the aisles, chapels, and the free-standing bell-tower were added later. The tall and graceful spire was finished in 1866, its predecessor having collapsed in 1861. Mr Alec Clifton-Taylor writes that he once spoke with an old man who told him he saw it happen, from a train window. The spire suddenly telescoped into itself.

It seems sad that so often the twentieth-century additions to a venerable building are the least harmonious: the Piper tapestry behind the high altar, and the Chagall window, do not yet appear to blend with their surroundings. There are monuments to the composer Gustav Holst, to William Huskisson, MP, the first railway casualty, and to a fifteenth-century Earl and Countess of Arundel, whose stone effigies, touchingly, are holding hands. There is also a fragment of Roman mosaic, found and now displayed, beneath the paving of the south aisle.

Chichester's *Festival Theatre*, in the park beyond the North walls, has just celebrated its twenty-fifth birthday: it may be an unusual building, but it has attracted to the city the best of actors in the finest productions over the years.

Chichester is near the sea. The air is fresh, gulls wheel and cry around its streets, and its cathedral spire, it is said, is the only one in England which can be seen by ships at sea.

Arundel Castle

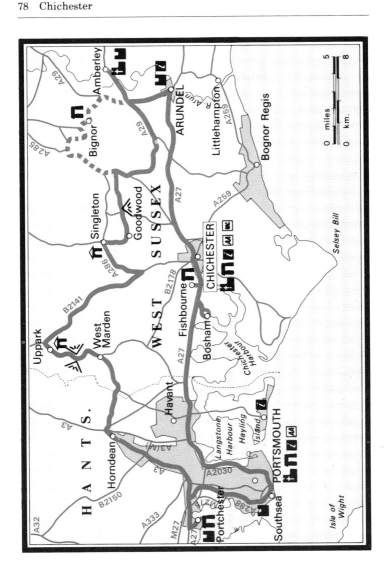

Chichester – Fishbourne – Bosham – Portsmouth – Porchester – Uppark – Singleton – Amberley – Arundel – Chichester

Tour length 82 miles

A maritime flavour is bound to blow about a tour which clings so much to a sea-coast. Relics from the past hang reciprocally all about that coast, from the astonishing Romano-British palace at Fishbourne, to the assortment of naval and military antiquities at Portsmouth, and to the 1,700-year-old walls of Portchester Castle. But for variety there are the hills and valleys of the hinterland, and an excellent exhibition at Singleton of the very earliest kinds of domestic houses to be found in the whole South-East, rebuilt as they were when new. Ships and castles, saltwater and greenwood, mud-flats and high hills play a part in this tour.

Fishbourne Not far out of Chichester, going west on the A27, a turning to the right takes you to the amazingly extensive and superbly preserved and presented Roman palace at Fishbourne. It came to light when a drain was being dug across a field, and no matter where the archaeologists (who appeared like wasps round a jam-jar) excavated, they found more. A huge permanent shelter, air-conditioned to a constant temperature, now covers it, and still there is obviously more underground.

The palace, as spacious and magnificent as any in Italy, is thought to have probably been that of King Cogidubnus, left by the Romans to rule Regnum, his southern kingdom, in acquiescent peace. It has bath-houses, under-floor heating, ovens, and in its reception rooms the . most graphic and colourful of mosaics, one in particular showing Cupid riding on a dolphin. They are the earliest known (first-century) mosaics in Britain. There are also traces of the people who lived there, to bring it all into touch with us: personal articles of dress, footprints on tiles, a skeleton lying where it was found.

A short way along the A27 another turning, this time to the left, will bring a very different

Bosham experience; it leads to Bosham, one of the villages on Chichester Harbour. The tidal inlets that penetrate this part of the South Coast, it is thought, are probably on a small scale what the waters about Pevensey, Rye, Oxney, and the Stour estuary used to be like. If the tide is out, there are wide mud-flats and a distant channel; if it is in, the boats bob in the water, the quays are hectic with movement, and on a fine day you might be in some Mediterranean waterfront village. Bosham itself is attractive, and of course is full of boats in gardens, yachtsmen and women in rubber boots, everywhere the smell of mud, seaweed, and salt, and probably the children are born with webbed feet. It is picturesque and immensely appealing.

There is naturally no way through Bosham, so you must return to the A27 and follow it, close to the heads of the watery channels, at Southbourne, Emsworth, and Langstone, where the road to Hayling Island crosses a long bridge to your left. Views appear now of the wide expanse **Langstone** of Langstone Harbour, which in the days of **Harbour** wooden ships was capable of giving anchorage to a large section of the fleet.

The scenery for the next several miles is not too appealing, because we are circling Portsmouth, which is no more gorgeous than any other dockyard town. First (having turned left at the head of Langstone Harbour on the A2030 and **Southsea** joined the A288) you pass through Southsea, where at Eastney stand the barracks and museum of the Royal Marines. Then comes the sea-front of Southsea, with some good-looking hotels on the pattern of Brighton and Eastbourne, and down on the sea-wall itself a castle kept in immaculate repair and used as a museum. Southsea Castle was one of those built by Henry VIII to improve coastal defences in the 1540s. From it the watchers in 1545 witnessed a disaster when the fleet turned to repel a French attack: the battleship *Mary Rose* capsized and sank with all hands. In 1982 after strenuous efforts to lift the wreck off the sea-bed it was placed in dry-dock: it has yielded a wonderful crop of objects and information about naval usages and conditions of the period, much of it previously unknown. The *Mary Rose* now lies alongside another, later battleship which served many years in the Navy and took part as flagship in one of its most significant actions.

If you follow the road to a junction opposite **Portsmouth** Portsmouth Cathedral (whose bell-tower has a faintly New England look about it) and turn right, past the bustling, crowded Old Harbour, full of lively activity, and then keep left, you come to the Royal Naval Dockyard and can visit that famous old wooden ship *HMS Victory*, a 100-gun line-of-battle ship in which Admiral Lord Nelson flew his flag in his last, and most urgent, battle. Aboard the ship, everything is kept in perfect trim, scrubbed and polished, and you will be conducted through it by a serving sailor, for *HMS Victory* is still commissioned, with officers and crew.

On the way out of the city on the A3 there is a Charles Dickens museum: the writer was born here in Portsmouth. Reverting to the A27 you can skirt the top of Portsmouth Harbour and **Portchester** turn off the road left to visit Portchester. At the very end of the village street you come to Portchester Castle, whose story is very similar to Pevensey's, but whose structure is in much better order. Like Pevensey it began as a Roman Saxon Shore fort, on the water's edge as a defence against pirates, and was adapted by the Normans 700 years later with a new castle built in one corner. Unlike Pevensey, the Roman walls enclose a rectangular space, and although patched are still substantially Roman and intact. The water washes up against them still, and the Norman keep in one corner is also in good repair, its stairs climbable and the superb view from the battlements obtainable. Furthermore there is a perfect little Norman chapel within the walls.

In the village street near the castle there is an inn called the *Cormorant*, which has a splendid buffet bar, and provided you enjoy pop music played very loudly while you eat and drink, this is the place for you.

To return from Portchester to the A27, back the way you came, and turn left on the A3 through the rather dreary suburbs of Waterlooville, Cowplain, and Horndean is not very exciting, but

the alternative is a maze of lanes in the hills,
scenically pleasant but frustratingly puzzling.

Horndean Leave the A3 at Horndean (you will not be sorry
by this time) right on the B2149, then turn off it
left almost at once by a lane, heading for
Finchdean and West Marden and ignoring
Rowlands Castle. The western South Downs are
much more wooded but just as precipitous as
their eastern fellows, and if you keep heading for
West Marden and Compton you will arrive at the
B2146, having experienced their scenic sub-
tleties. Turn left and keep climbing, taking a
quick glance when feasible at the landscape,
which is a feast for the senses after the
Portsmouth area's dullness: masses of stately
trees, woods tumbling down every hillside, green
pasture in the narrow ravines.

Uppark Eventually you come to the drive to Uppark
(well-named, this) which is a fairly small but
elegant house built in 1790, with its mid-
eighteenth-century furnishings and hangings
almost complete. As it is so high, there are
splendid views all round. If you continue on the
B2146, quite soon you come to its junction with
the B2141 (be careful, because the roads meet at
the bottom of a very steep hill); turn sharp right
on it and follow its winding course up and over
Marden Forest and down to the deep valley
below it. Visibility hereabouts is limited because
the trees are so close-set, and habitations are
few. The road now follows the narrow valley
bottom, and you can see how Marden Forest
crowds and hangs over the whole western hill-

Chilgrove side. At Chilgrove there is a good inn, and
several miles farther on there is the junction
with the main A286 road. You are not far from
Chichester here, and you have travelled through
the kind of semi-mountainous forested scenery
that is on its doorstep.

Turn left on the A286 through West Dean, and

Singleton at Singleton take a right turn signposted to the
Weald and Downland Open Air Museum. This
extraordinary display occupies a whole side of
the valley and exhibits a remarkable collection
of historic buildings. These have been rescued,
often from destruction of some kind such as
immersion in a reservoir, taken down, trans-

ported here, and reconstructed as nearly as when they were first built as possible. They are not all dwelling houses, for they include a water-mill (which works), a treadwheel, a forge, carpenter's and plumber's workshops, a charcoal-burner's hut and camp and apparatus, and sundry barns and corn-stores. Among the houses there is a very early medieval farmhouse, and a Wealden hall-house, like many you have already seen in Kent and East Sussex but without modern additions such as chimneys and window glass.

Goodwood If you continue on the lane past the museum's entrance, climbing up the hillside again, you will come to the famous Goodwood racecourse. Turn left past it along a lane in which there are places for parking and picnicking, and you can join those already doing so in enjoying the sensational view of the open country to the south down to Chichester and the sea.

The lane leads you gently down to the main A285 road, and there are two alternatives, depending on time available and whether or not you are in the mood for another Roman villa and a trek like Livingstone's into the African bush to get to it. First the easy way, missing the Roman villa at Bignor: turn right on the A285, then left Eartham on lanes to Eartham and Slindon, which bring you shortly to the A29. Turn left on it and head for Amberley.

If you fancy the Bignor alternative, turn left on the A285 and climb up and over the Downs. As you come flying down a hairpin bend towards Duncton, clap on the brakes and shoot off right to a lane which proclaims that it is one way. This is just as well, because if you met even a chicken coming the other way, it could be nasty. This very narrow lane squeezes between trees and high hedges, and ejects you first to the hamlet of Bignor Sutton, and then to Bignor (where incidentally, there is a hall-house in marvellous condition, thatched, with flint-and-brick in-filling between its oak timbers). The Roman villa is signposted, and you take a long track on the left across the fields to reach it. The villa is preserved under thatched sheds in parts, and is therefore more difficult to comprehend in its entirety than Fishbourne or Lullingstone, but it was evidently

large and sumptuous, with more fine mosaics. It
lies near the course of the road which ran from
Chichester to London, called by the Saxons
Stane Street, at the tenth Roman mile from
Chichester. There is a quantity of the same kind
of personal articles, pins and pots and buckles
and bowls, as are found in most Roman sites. It is
well worth the visit, if your nerves can stand the
course. Your lane goes on to the A29 and you
have to turn right, then left at the junction with
the B2139 road to Amberley.

Houghton The road descends very steeply to the river
plain of the Arun, and a long bridge at Houghton
to cross it. You are on the north side of the gap
made by the river through the Downs, and the
Amberley small castle at Amberley, never much more than
a fortified manor-house built by a fourteenth-
century bishop of Chichester, surveys a watery,
grassy plain called Amberley Wild Brooks. The
village, lying uncoordinatedly to the east of this
walled house, and of the church, is delightful. Its
houses, whether of stone, brick, or timber, tiled
or thatched, are all different from each other.

Returning up the steep hill beyond the ancient
Houghton bridge, turn left at the A29 junction to
the A284 road, which skirts the wall of the great
Arundel estate. Turn off it left to the head of the
Arundel town of Arundel and the mighty gatehouse to the
castle. It might by this time be too late to enter,
for the last admissions are at 4pm. However, it is
worth knowing that this seat of the Dukes of
Norfolk is basically a Norman fortress, built to
guard the Arun gap just as Lewes was to defend
the Ouse valley. Parts of the original castle still
stand, but a large part dates from the nineteenth
century. Ownership, through the Howards,
Dukes of Norfolk, can be traced back in the same
family to William de Albini, who was granted the
castle in 1138.

The A27 will take you back the 10 miles to
Chichester.

Winchester

Tourist Information Office
City Offices, Colebrook Street, tel 65406 (weekends 68166)

Population 31.070

Cinema
Studios 1, 2 & 3, North Walls.

Museums
City Museum, Market Street
Westgate Museum, High Street
Royal Greenjackets Museum
Royal Hussars Museum

Places of Interest

Cathedral	King's Gate
Great Hall	West Gate
Pilgrims' Hall	St John's Church

Like Chichester and Canterbury, Winchester was a town before it was even a Roman army camp. As *Venta Belgarum* it radiated the southern road system, controlling the coastal traffic up Southampton Water and the Itchen, with its port at Bitterne. It became, without much interruption, the chief city of the West Saxons, and when their kings were the only English monarchs left, of the English. Only in the twelfth century did the Royal Treasury move to London.

Lying on the side of the hill, the castle at the top and the River Itchen at the bottom, the city retains its rectangular shape and is bisected by its High Street, from top to bottom. Beginning at the Guildhall, a mighty Victorian building with an overpowering clock-tower, two things are visible to your right: one, a statue of King Alfred the Great in the middle of the street before it crosses the river; the other, a little thirteenth-century chapel just opposite belonging to St John's Hospital, around the corner. Up the High Street, near the City Cross, lanes lead off left into the Square, where the City Museum stands on a corner, and the great Cathedral lies in its quiet green precinct. It is unobtrusive, in that it has no great spire or tower to dominate the city: it is very long, stately, and grey, and magnificent. Inside the west door, where you enter, you can look down the whole length of the nave, a stone forest of tall trees, their branches linking overhead in the fan vaulting. There is a huge carved wooden screen, with choir stalls behind, and a massive reredos beyond the high altar which looks like intricately carved stone but is actually also wood, painted to resemble stone. There are shrines to favourite bishops, such as William of Wykeham, founder of Winchester College. Above the choir stalls, lying on the wooden screens, there are mortuary chests containing relics of early Wessex kings from the seventh century on, but as the Roundhead soldiers of the Civil War thought they were treasure chests and broke them open, the bones got somewhat mixed up. The transepts are pure Norman, three-tier like Chichester's nave. Here, in this old, old place, are grandeur and dignity, peace and wisdom. Here in 1100 was buried fierce King William Rufus; here in 1817 too, gentle Jane Austen.

Turn sharp right from the west door, around the side of the Cathedral's north wall, and enter the precinct close to the ancient deanery. Before you, across the still square, is a long timber-framed, two-storey building, plastered between the beams in the upper storey, brick in-filled below: this is Pilgrim's Hall. Close by it is King's Gate, with little St Swithin's chapel above it, over the gateway. On its far side is College Street, to your left, and in No. 8 the novelist Jane Austen died. To your right is Canon Street, leading to Southgate Street, from which Cromwell's gunners pounded away at the castle at the top of the city until there was little left of it.

At the end of Southgate Street turn left up the hill to Westgate, a fortified gateway of the fourteenth century. Above it on the castle's site are the Council Offices and the last vestiges, just uncovered, of the castle's masonry.

In most castles, the great hall is the first building to disappear: at Winchester, it is the only remaining part above ground. The Great Hall, much patched and renovated, has a fine timbered roof, and at one end hangs a circular wooden object, painted in alternate blue and white, called the Round Table. It bears the names of King Arthur's knights, and some people will swear that it is the genuine article used by those worthies. Some people will believe anything.

Winchester – Romsey – Mottisfont – King's Somborne – Stockbridge – Micheldever – Alresford – Chawton – Selborne – Winchester

Tour length 82 miles

The lovely rivers Test and Itchen flow to west and east of Winchester, springing from the hills to the north, which are the western end of the North Downs. The whole area is criss-crossed with arterial roads, converging on Winchester or the great port of Southampton, but between the roads lies some of the least-trodden country in southern England. Except in the valleys, it is not a country either for castles or great houses, but it is certainly for retiring and observant writers.

Straight up the High Street hill in Winchester, past the Council Offices and the Depot of the Royal Greenjackets, the city roads lead out to the A31 and the way to Romsey. All the way, as the road is alternately straight and fast, then twisting like an eel, cool greenwood abounds on both sides.

Romsey   It is very difficult to get into Romsey from the A31. The one-way system leads you towards the town centre, but the street which clearly goes straight into it is 'No entry', and at once you are turned out again. What you have to do, after turning right on the A3057, the Stockbridge Road, is to turn off right again to a car park; you can then penetrate the mystery on foot.

Romsey Abbey is the church of a nunnery, founded in 907. It was burnt down by the Vikings in 990 and rebuilt in 999. Another extensive rebuilding followed in 1120, which is why it presents a typical Norman Romanesque appearance, high, wide, massive, and stately. The nunnery, of course, disappeared at the Dissolution. The church was offered by Henry VIII (or, perhaps, by his cynical Secretary, Thomas Cromwell) to the townsmen of Romsey, for £100. They bought it, and have had to maintain it, without any other financial support, ever since.

Nearby a tiny flint building is called King

ALTON
Chawton
Selborne
Ropley
Petersfield
A31
A339
A32
B3046
Old Alresford
NEW ALRESFORD
Northington
A272
R. Itchen
A31
HAMPSHIRE
Micheldever
A33
A34
B3420
A272
A30
Sutton Scotney
A333
WINCHESTER
A3090
A31
A333
ROMSEY
King's Somborne
R. Test
A3057
Mottisfont
A31
Stockbridge
A272
A3057
A27
B3084

miles 0   5
km. 0   8

John's House, because that monarch is supposed to have stayed in it. Parts of it are clearly medieval, but it is much bricked up and patched, and the lop-sided timbered cottage at one end can hardly be from the early thirteenth century. They will tell you for sure inside, because it houses the Tourist Information Office.

Broadlands Opposite the end of the road by which the one-way system throws you out of the town, is the drive to Broadlands, a great eighteenth-century house in beautiful parkland, which was the home of the late Earl Mountbatten. If not well known for that, at least the whole nation will be aware that the present Prince of Wales and his bride went there on the evening of their wedding day, 29 July 1981. Some (but rather fewer, perhaps) might also be aware that it was once the home of the inimitable Lord Palmerston (a statue of whom stands in the town square in Romsey) until he died in 1865.

The A3057 road to Stockbridge follows the eastern side of the Test valley, but has to cross it several times because the Test has a multiplicity of streams. A turning left crosses all of them on **Mottisfont** its way to Mottisfont, where sometimes you may be able to see the grand house converted after the Dissolution from the church of Mottisfont Abbey. A brick front was erected in the eighteenth century, and the result, an amalgam of work from totally different periods, is unique. The grounds, with a branch of the river running through, are like those of Broadlands, delightful. From Mottisfont a lane follows the river northward, for the most part undisturbed by traffic; about you is a gentle, comforting blanket of green, in all the shades of the woods and fields, hedges and verges.

Houghton At Houghton the lane turns right and crosses the manifold streams of the river. The Test, coming from the North Downs, is a chalk stream like the Kentish Stour. It is shallow, crystal clear, and has a reputation for trout. To stand at one of the bridges, gazing into the water, seeing it swirling, making curves and arabesques, wafting the water-plants to follow it, plaiting the sunshine into patterns of colours, pondering perhaps the anomalous mystery of rivers, always

the same yet always different, like each successive day of life: it is occasionally an occupation
that produces a rare truth, because this same
anomaly, of placid stillness arising from swift
movement, seems to exert the power of making
one think.

By the last of the streams there is an old brick
mill, half obscured by a huge weeping willow,
with an inn adjacent. If you fork left at the inn
you return to the A3057 and, keeping left, soon
King's   arrive in King's Somborne. Although you may
Somborne   already have paused frequently in this time-
ignoring Test landscape, there may be a temp-
tation to do so again here, because the green,
with war memorial and nearby church, is fringed
with old, mainly thatched cottages, one of them
an inn called the *Crown*. In composition it is
another of those essentially English scenes, like
Woodchurch and Benenden in Kent.

Thatch is still very much in use hereabouts, and
some of the more ruinous thatches can often be
contrasted with others new and yellow. I once
met a thatcher in an inn at Longstock, the other
side of the Test, who was not short of work.

Stockbridge   Stockbridge, which you next approach on this
road, is a market town, and although the name
may not have quite that derivation, it is certainly
a bridge across which stock used to be driven on
their way from the west country up to the rich
markets of London. On the lane the other side of
the river from Houghton, there used to be a
cottage with a faintly discernible advertisement
painted across it, for good lodging, beer, and hay:
in Welsh. Many of the drovers brought their
stock all the way from South Wales. This A3057
road does not really touch more than the edge of
the town; you need to turn left to the streets on
either side of the bridge to see it properly.

Tempting though it is to linger (for ever?) in the
vicinity of the Test's cool, sweet streams, it is
time to turn away from it and seek the hills.
From Stockbridge, take the A30 road for a long,
straight stretch over the hills between the Test
and Itchen valleys, a high ridge offering rich
views of the lovely, lush Hampshire landscape.
Sutton   At Sutton Scotney the road is joined by the A34.
Scotney   Turn right on it, then immediately left by the

little church on a lane that follows a tributary to the Test. It takes you through the villages of Wonston, Stoke Charity, and Micheldever, all in placid pastoral and arboreal settings, with some of the most attractive of the vernacular brick-timber-and-thatched cottages, made bright with flowers. Unlike such places as Alfriston which expect crowds of visitors, Micheldever for instance has no free car park, and its inn, the *Half Moon and Spread Eagle*, caters principally for local customers. There can be few complaints.

The lane past the inn leads to the A33 which, since it started life as a Roman *via strata* to their cantonal capital *Venta Belgarum* (Winchester), describes the shortest distance between two points. Turn off it soon, however, left on a lane by the *Lunways Inn*, signposted Northington. This is forest country among the hills, with Micheldever Wood on one side and Itchen Wood on the other, both controlled by the Forestry Commission with allotted places for car-parking and picnicking visitors. This is not the New Forest, however, and woods such as these doubtless have depths which very seldom experience a human footfall.

At Northington turn right on the B3046 road to Alresford. Old and New Alresford are like Old and New Romney: neither predates the other and the terms are used only for differentiation. In both cases, however, New is bigger. Old Alresford is a scattering of houses, with a brick eighteenth-century church and a big house, now the headquarters of the Winchester Diocesan Synod. It all stands above or beside a mighty embankment along which the road runs. Below it the waters of the little River Alre are channelled to feed a mill and a large expanse of water, with another on the higher side. This embankment is not new; it was engineered in the twelfth century for commercial purposes by the energetic Bishop de Lucy of Winchester. Its only products today appear to be watercress, ducks, coots, and mosquitoes.

New Alresford is an equally aged village, its houses beginning at the southern end of the embankment, but it has grown into a town, despite having been burnt down by Royalist

Micheldever

Old Alresford

New Alresford

forces during the Civil War, and by accident in 1689. Few of its houses, therefore, are older than that date, but many, with their well-proportioned Georgian fronts, remain from the rebuilding during the next thirty or forty years. The T-junction of streets are wide and handsome, and although the town has spread with modern development to the south, these streets retain their country-town character.

The main A31 road forms the cross-piece of the New Alresford T. Turn left on it and go a few miles, in the course of which you may see much of this pleasant Hampshire countryside, with views to either side and plenty of attractive villages on the way, such as Bishops Sutton, North Street, and Four Marks. At the round-about where the A32 joins the road, there is a

Chawton lane signposted to Chawton and Jane Austen's house. Chawton in fact is bypassed by the road, for which it is no doubt thankful, and the small brick house on the corner of its street is where our first eminent lady novelist lived, from 1809 until the year she died, 1817. Her brother Edward inherited property including Chawton House, which necessitated changing his name to Knight. He provided his mother and unmarried sisters, Jane and Cassandra, with this comfortable small house in the village. Jane wrote her last three books here, unostentatiously, at a little circular table kept in the dining-room, on easily hidden small sheets of paper. The house has several rooms filled with letters, family portraits, mementoes, manuscripts, and a published diagnosis, from the scanty evidence (mainly supplied by Jane herself in letters), in the *British Medical Journal*, of the obscure disease which killed her at such a distressingly early age (41). Anyone who has read and relished Jane's books can hardly fail to find plenty to intrigue them in this well-presented exhibition.

At the end of the pretty village street the lane turns sharp right and leads soon to the B3006 and the hill country, where ridge tops are covered with flourishing beech woods. The pretty but

Selborne otherwise undistinguished village of Selborne, tucked away at the bottom of one of these deep secretive valleys, has been rendered famous because a quiet, retiring curate, the Rev Gilbert White, lived here all his life and wrote exhaustively and observantly about 'natural productions and occurrences'. His home, 'The Wakes', has been made a Gilbert White Museum, a nearby bookshop sells all the editions of his work available, and the better to accommodate visitors there is that mark of distinction, so welcome a sight to motorists, a free car park.

'The high part to the south-west', White writes, 'consists of a vast hill of chalk, rising three hundred feet above the village; and is divided into a sheep-down, the high wood, and a long hanging wood, called the Hanger. The covert of this eminence is altogether beech, the most lovely of all forest trees, whether we consider its smooth rind or bark, its glossy foliage, or graceful pendulous boughs.'

Well marked paths can take you up to the Hanger, and a variety of stuffed animals and birds in the Wakes museum, with comprehensive comparisons of White's findings with current conditions (which do not seem to have changed all that much since his time, the second half of the eighteenth century), can occupy you for hours. White's *Natural History of Selborne* covers a remarkable field of observations on subjects as diverse as rabbits and ravens, bees and bats, echoes and cuckoos, frogs and worms, and all kinds of birds imaginable.

Upstairs in the Wakes, as a kind of bonus, are exhibitions of the life and work of two members of the Oates family, who bought the house. Frank explored in Africa, where he died of a fever, and Lawrence explored in the Antarctic, where he died in a vain attempt to make it possible for Captain Scott and the others to survive. More stuffed animals and birds accompany these displays.

It is important to take the first lane to the right at the end of the village street (still going south) which is signposted to Newton Valence. If you miss it and take a later one, you will probably spend the rest of the day (if not the rest of your life) wandering endlessly around the fearfully narrow, twisting, hollow ways of this piece of nearly deserted country. A hollow way, many of

which exist in southern England, is an old lane,
once used by pack-horse trains, so worn that it is
sunk in a gully, with trees on either side meeting
over the top like the vaults at the top of the nave
columns in Winchester Cathedral, but claustro-
phobically lower. Smugglers used to utilise lanes
like these because they could travel unseen
along them.

The correct lane brings you across this extremely unfrequented stretch of South-East
England to the main A32 road: turn left on it,
Ropley and quite soon right on a lane to Ropley. It
appears to go on for ever, even after passing
through Ropley, but the process is enjoyable
because the scenery is so completely and relax-
ingly tranquil (30 miles per hour is the maximum
speed possible, on the straight, because the road
is so narrow). Eventually you arrive on the A31
near New Alresford, and if you turn left you can
travel along it for a few miles and return to
Winchester.

Lyndhurst

Tourist Information Office
Caravan in free car park

Population 3,180

Places of Interest
Church
New Forest

The chief object in choosing Lyndhurst as a centre for touring the New Forest is that it has some good hotels, and stands in the centre of the road system that serves the area, which makes the prescription of a comprehensive tour that much easier.

The bulk of the town's building, certainly in the High Street which ascends the northward hill, dates from the turn of the nineteenth and twentieth centuries, not unfortunately a period that enjoyed the greatest felicity of style. The church is earlier, a representative of the most strident form of Victorian ecclesiastical architecture, in an assortment of coloured brick guaranteed never to mellow. Inside it, however, are some excellent windows by the best late Victorian artists, such as Burne-Jones, William Morris, Ford Madox Brown and Rossetti, which make it worth visiting for their sake.

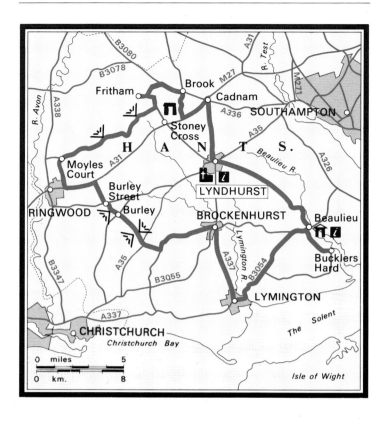

Lyndhurst – Rufus Stone – Fritham – Moyles Court – Burley – Brockenhurst – Lymington – Beaulieu – Lyndhurst –

Tour length 65 miles

The New Forest, like New Romney and New Alresford, is not of a similar vintage to, say, New York or New Zealand. An inhospitable wilderness from earliest times, it was created a royal forest by King William the Conqueror, whose favourite sport was hunting the red deer. Severe penalties were visited on anyone caught poaching in it, and the outcome was that the Forest laws were sufficient to prevent the Forest from being encroached on by other kinds of poacher, such as agricultural-ists or land-developers. Now, although the Forest is a major attraction to hikers, pony-trekkers, campers, caravanners, naturalists, and just motorised visitors like ourselves, their impact on it is really merely peripheral: so vast an area may absorb them all without undue disturbance, and the Forestry Commission enforce their own Forest laws with vigilance. Go into the Forest and you will soon lose the visitors: I once walked from Burley to Stoney Cross along the Forest ways, in the high season, and met no one except on the crossing roads.

Cadnam Go north from Lyndhurst on the A337 to the big roundabout at Cadnam, and despite a notice when you turn left on the A31 that says 'No right turns for 8 miles', follow it because there is one after about two, signposted to Rufus Stone. As soon as you leave the main road the symptoms of a typical Forest road appear: the lane is narrow, lined with outcrops of sandy stone, with heather and bracken, it twists and turns, and there are encounters with wandering animals, usually ponies. Within a mile or so there is a gravelled car park of the kind that have been marked out and provided all over the Forest, and across the **Rufus Stone** grass under some trees you will see a triangular pedestal (not a pyramid, a small three-sided column), faced with iron and bearing on each of the three sides a part of the story of the mysterious death of King William II.

The sons of William the Conqueror were all vile, and William, called Rufus because of his ruddy complexion, was the vilest. He ruled for 13 years with violence and tyranny, detested by his barons and by the Church, which he regarded with contempt, but somewhat admired by the conquered English, who preferred a strong king to rapacious barons (including bishops and abbots). As fond of the chase as his father, he was on 2 August 1100 engaged in his favourite pursuit when, on this spot, he was apparently accidentally killed by a stray shot from his companion, a Norman knight called Walter Tyrell or Tirel. His brother Henry, another member of the hunting party but not present at the scene, when told the news made off at once to seize the royal treasury at Winchester, and was crowned king at Westminster within three days. Tirel had bolted abroad. The Rufus Stone's inscription calls the event an accident: but Henry's actions make one suspicious, to say the least.

The Forest, devoid of all signs of our motorised age, probably looked much the same then, and standing in the sunlight as it dapples the grass through the green oak-leaves, it is hard to conjure up the image of sudden death, assassination, and political chicanery. Better to pursue **Brook** the lane past the Stone to Brook, turning left along the B3078 for a short way, fringed by dense greenwood, with a grassy verge on both sides, then turn left again, and right to Fritham.

There are not many villages in the Forest. There is an old and malign legend that King William destroyed thirty villages with their parish churches, evicting their occupants, to create his great deer-forest. It persists, despite William Cobbett, the outspoken radical journalist of the time of the wars against Napoleonic France, who pointed out that the Forest's thick clay, loose sand, gravels, and marls had never been fertile in all its history, and could not possibly have supported thirty parishes. In fact, their existence would have made the Forest the most densely populated area in the whole of England, which defied all logic. No doubt, he concluded, the legend was fabricated by the natives' hatred of the harsh Forest laws, which prevented their traditional freedom to hunt there.

Fritham Fritham is strung out along a lane which comes

to an end at a wide green (with another car
park), with a scattering of cottages, an inn, and
some attendant animals. Thereafter, only tracks
lead off into the jungle, because Fritham is on
the fringe of a vast swathe of thickly wooded
forest-land, whose subtle emanation of scented,
secret silence can be sensed from the quiet green.

The Forest, however, is not all trees: returning
along Fritham's lane to where you turned off,
and going right, you come to an immense plain
Janesmoor called Janesmoor, with the edge of the trees in
the distance, a tract of grass and heather, often
full of horses, either hacks being ridden or
clusters of the wild Forest ponies. The prolifera-
tion of these animals means that, even on this
road, or on the one that goes off to the right
across the plain, straight and open so that
visibility is clear, a modest speed must be
observed, because you never know when a group
of these creatures will saunter into the road and
stand immobile, waving their heads and tails
about to whisk the flies, watching you crawl
round them in bottom gear. Also, like most of the
minor Forest lanes, this one is narrow, with only
just room for two vehicles. Caution is essential
on these two counts, quite apart from the pleasure to be derived from looking at the scenery.

Here, on this lane through Janesmoor, and on
to the north-western section of the Forest, the
hills are purple with heather and trees are
relatively scarce. Distant stands of woodland do
not impede far views of rolling, undulating
heather banks, with blue-green forest in the
farthest hills and vales. You begin to realise the
immensity of this wilderness.

The woodland returns as the lane dips and
wriggles its way to Linwood and Moyles Court,
and a turning left at the latter hamlet brings you
to the A31 on the right side of Ringwood. Turn
left on it, and right quite soon at Picket Post on
the way to Burley. On this road again the
heights, unobstructed, give commanding views
all around of near and distant parts of this vast
forest, its character varying from heathland to
woodland, and the woods from greenwood to
conifer. Burley Street is a hamlet on its own, and
several wriggles have to be negotiated before

Burley   reaching Burley, which like Lyndhurst seems to owe much to the days of King Edward VII. It has a large inn, the *Queen's Head*, and on the hilltop ahead, a cricket ground.

Between Burley and Stoney Cross, where the A31 crosses Janesmoor, is some of the densest woodland of all, and if you care to sample it then Burley Lawn   follow the lane past the *Queen's Head* to Burley Lawn. You will have to leave the car, because within the Forestry Commission's enclosures no vehicles are permitted, nor is camping, lighting fires, dropping litter, nor any form of persecution of wildlife. This means that quite often you are entirely on your own and may walk for miles in perfect solitude and peace. If you do this, you may form a far better impression of the real Forest than at most other places, because away from any contact with twentieth-century manners and methods, you may listen to the silence: a palpable silence filled with faint sound, of the surf-like wind surging in the treetops, of the humming of a million insects, of a thousand invisible birds chanting their orisons. You may breathe in the hundred unidentifiable scents of woodland and soil, you may taste the golden water in the little streams and you may rest your eyes on the soft kaleidoscope of changing greens and yellows, russets, and browns all about you. To be in the Forest's impregnable depths is like being solitary on a mountain-top: there is room, and time, to think.

The road through Burley and its cricket ground leads to the southern part of the forest and the Brockenhurst   village of Brockenhurst. Here again there are wide spaces without trees, acres of heather and gorse and bracken, ridges and valleys. Brockenhurst, although southerly, is an alternative to Lyndhurst as a base, because roads meet at it, there is a railway station, and it has hotels. The A337 road from Lyndhurst runs through it, and if followed farther south leads you to Lymington, still with traces of the Forest and still with the possibility of meeting a swarm of ponies round every corner.

Lymington   Lymington has a dual function because, lying on the edge of the Forest it caters for visitors to it, but it also has a river, into which drain many of the little Forest streams, and the river meets the Solent, so it is also a maritime town. Its High Street dips sharply, narrowing at the lower end, and you must turn right to go to the riverside, where anchorage is available for numerous yachts. The Solent and its tributary rivers constitute the best of South-East England's yachting waters.

The B3054 road leads out of Lymington across another stretch of heathland to Beaulieu, but a short way before the village a lane turns right to **Bucklers** a curious phenomenon called Bucklers Hard. The **Hard** Montagu family has owned the Beaulieu estate since 1667, and the 2nd Duke of Montagu developed a project, in the estuary of the Beaulieu river, for receiving and distributing the sugar produce of his West Indian island of Lucia. The plans included docks and a whole new town, but only two rows of cottages were built before the project folded up. However, the Hard later became a shipbuilding yard, using material from the nearby forests, and some of the great wooden battleships of the Royal Navy, including *HMS Agamemnon*, one of Lord Nelson's flagships, were built and launched into the deep estuary waters. The Montagu family still owns the estate, and to visit Bucklers Hard today, some of whose cottages have been made into a Maritime Museum, you must stop in the car park and pay the required fee before you can even see the water.

Beaulieu   King John is generally regarded as much of an enemy of the Church as Rufus (mainly because it was rich and he needed money, so he overtaxed it), but it was he who founded a Cistercian monastery in this suitably deserted *Bellus Locus Regi*, with large estates for its upkeep in the fertile farmlands of the estuary, and elsewhere in rich southern England. It was not completed until well after his time, but the abbey became rich and was eagerly bought at the Dissolution by Thomas Wriothesley, later Henry VIII's Lord Chancellor. The abbey buildings fell into disrepair, except for the refectory, which became the parish church, and the huge gatehouse, made into a residence. The latter was turned into the form Palace House takes today by a son of the

5th Duke of Buccleuch (another branch of the same Montagu family), who was given the estate by his father as a wedding present.

The present Lord Montagu, a motoring enthusiast, has developed an enormous Motor Museum, opened Palace House, and furnished in the gardens of his estate sufficient other entertainments and attractions to occupy visitors (and their children) all day. According to the advertising leaflet, 'Beaulieu is an experience that stays with you long after you leave. THE great day out. The charm of Palace House, the history of the motor car shown in a thousand ways in the Motor Museum, the quiet peace of the Abbey and Monastic Exhibition, will be recalled and enjoyed for years to come. Add to this exciting memories of the Monorail, the Veteran Bus, the Model Railway and the other Special Features that go on through the long season, making Beaulieu unforgettable in every way.'

Although King John might be surprised at the subsequent development of his foundation, not to say irritated, there is no doubt that it offers plenty for you to do and see.

From the pretty roadside view across a mere, the village roofs on your right, and the topmost turrets of Palace House, flag flying, rearing above the trees to your left, making reflections in the water, the B3056 road leads northward, past the estate entrance, back through the Forest greenwood to Lyndhurst.

Guildford

Tourist Information Office
Central Library, North Street, tel 68496

Population 58,470

Theatre
Yvonne Arnaud Theatre, Riverside

Cinemas
Odeon, Epsom Road
Studios 1 & 2, Onslow Street

Museum
Castle Arch Museum

Places of Interest
Grammar School
Abbott's Hospital
Guildford House
Guildhall

Castle
St Mary's Church
Cathedral

Guildford is the modern county town of Surrey, long its administrative centre, like Maidstone for Kent, and only recently also an ecclesiastical and academic centre. It owes its origin to a ford across the River Wey, at the foot of the High Street, and the existence of the Saxon tower of St Mary's Church nearby demonstrates a stage in the antiquity of that origin. The Norman castle was built to guard the gap in the North Downs made by the Wey.

The steep cobbled High Street runs straight up from the riverside, and the majority of Guildford's historical buildings are clustered round it. At the top is the stone sixteenth-century Royal Grammar School, founded by young Edward VI. At the corner of the junction of North Street is the ancient Archbishop Abbott's Hospital, also from the sixteenth century but in brick, almshouses whose brothers and sisters are dressed in local blue woollen cloth, for the protection of Guildford weavers: opposite is Holy Trinity Church, rebuilt in the eighteenth century. Down from the Hospital is Guildford House, built in 1660, where art exhibitions are often held. Below that is the seventeenth-century Guildhall, with its famous clock of 1683 that projects over the street.

Down the hill on the left Quarry Street leads off and you can find there Castle Arch (housing a museum) admitting you to six acres of gardens and the jagged stump of the once-great

Norman keep, with walls fifteen feet thick at the base. A tiny alley off Quarry Street, called Rosemary Alley, consists of 29 steps and is so narrow the roofs almost touch. Nearby in Quarry Street is the old St Mary's Church, its Saxon tower proclaiming its seniority, but it also has what used to be a rare tri-apsidal east end, one apse of it now missing, with traces of medieval mural paintings in the remaining two.

Other houses in this oldest and therefore most interesting part of Guildford may claim attention, such as the Angel Hotel, the only remaining coaching inn, whose vaults are said to date from the early thirteenth century. The Guildhall displays its splendid regalia, the silver mace of the fifteenth century, the state sword and mayor's staff presented in the sixteenth.

Charles Dickens called it 'the most beautiful High Street in England': you must judge for yourself.

Guildford – Godalming – Hindhead – Haslemere – Midhurst – Petworth – Chiddingfold – Dunsfold – Leith Hill – Dorking – Polesden Lacey – Guildford

Tour length 85 miles

Surrey is often considered merely to be a sprawling extension of London, an unending suburb with no pretensions to true countryside. This perhaps could be said of Surrey north of the Downs, within reach of the Thames Valley, but it is certainly not true of southern Surrey. The North Downs, their formidable spur south as far as Haslemere, and the great basin of the Western Weald between North and South Downs contain some of the wildest and most spectacular scenery in the South-East. As in West Kent, proximity to London permits easy access to the wealthy, so there are great houses. There are also enchanting villages which might, from the look of them, be a hundred miles or more from reach of the capital.

Godalming

The A3100 road follows the River Wey south of Guildford to the pleasant town of Godalming, rejoins the A3 at Milford, and takes you into the heights of the remarkable stretch of wild heathland and forest that extends to Hindhead. It is not easy to see it from the A3 road, because it is usually somewhat busy, but there are occasional **Gibbet Hill** lay-bys and at the top of Gibbet Hill you are nearly 900 feet above sea level, overlooking an almost uninhabited vale called the Devil's Punch-Bowl. Views all around, reminiscent of the New Forest, are in some ways more dramatic than the gentle undulations of south-west Hampshire, because there are high peaks, crowned with ragged, serrated pine-woods, and deep, dark ravines in between. Admittedly, William Cobbett looked for fertility in a landscape, the best utilised by man, but he thought Gibbet Hill (a grim enough name) was 'the most villainous spot God ever made.' Try to walk away from the frantic clamour of the road, shutting your ears to the noise, and then perhaps some of the sheer romantic beauty of the place will appeal to you, even if it eluded Cobbett.

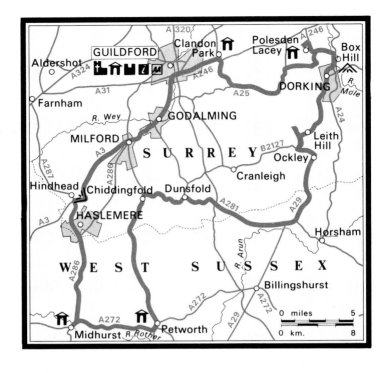

From Gibbet Hill the road descends sharply to
Hindhead Hindhead: turn left here on the A287, a short
Haslemere distance to Haslemere, where you can turn off
right on the A286, running gradually down from
the heathery coniferous heights into the rolling
greenwood of Sussex, for Haslemere is the last
town in Surrey.

Midhurst Midhurst is a little, unspoilt Sussex town of the
western Weald, in the valley of another River
Rother, a tributary to the Arun. As you approach
it from Easebourne, where the A272 joins your
road, you can see lying across the water-
meadows to your left the gaunt skeleton of a
ruined house. This is Cowdray, a magnificent
palace of Henry VIII's time which was burnt
down in 1793 and so badly damaged that it was
never rebuilt. Neither, however, was it demolished, and a new house was built nearby. The
park has become a famous centre for polo, which
brings some exceedingly important people to
visit it and play the game.

The town has a pleasant wide street with
substantial small houses ranging from the seventeenth to the nineteenth centuries, and behind
the High Street there is a charming Market
Square with a cross and some aged inns. Antique
shops abound, nor is there any difficulty in
finding coffee or tea shops.

This excursion into the Sussex Weald, with the
great hills of the South Downs ever visible on the
southern horizon, can be continued by following
the A272 eastward from Midhurst, along the
Petworth northern bank of the Rother to Petworth, a
smaller town all on a steep slope down to the
river, and dominated by the looming gates of
Petworth House, whose wall you have been
following, enclosing a huge area of deer-park, for
some way. Petworth is smaller, and prettier, than
Midhurst, with some large and imposing
eighteenth-century town houses and a few alleys,
such as Lombard Street between the Market
Square and the church, full of old stone or brick
cottages. From the street opposite the church, at
the top of the town, the big house behind its huge
gates looks greyly forbidding but in it you may
see a fine collection of paintings and furniture,
and some wood-carving by the illustrious

Grinling Gibbons. The deer-park is vast, and is accessible without charge all day, every day.

Above the little Rother valley the hills are very thickly wooded, with the typical Wealden mixture of oak, ash, thorn, and beech. The A283 road from Petworth takes you back through this pleasant landscape, rising again to cross the Surrey border east of Haslemere. A mile or two from the border, still on the A283, you come to

Chiddingfold the wide green of Chiddingfold, on the near corner of which stands the famous old *Crown Inn*, a wonderful timbered house with a renowned reputation.

If you turn right a short way past the green, a network of lanes will take you into some

Dunsfold thoroughly rustic country to Dunsfold, a village scattered in all directions around a large green, with a good inn to one side and dense woodland all around. In my opening paragraph to this tour I referred to wild and spectacular scenery in supposedly wholly domesticated Surrey. This Dunsfold region, with the extremely wild but better known Hindhead Common and Devil's Punch-Bowl, is the kind I meant: it looks like the remotest corner of the island, yet it is within (as the crow flies) 35 miles of Charing Cross. The inn, called the *Sun*, is an old timbered house, brick-fronted in the eighteenth century, which has been an inn for most of its existence. The woodland surrounding it is extensive and deep, and the lane winds sinuously through it as though unsure of the way.

It comes eventually to the A281 at its junction with the B2133. Ignore the latter and follow the former in the direction of Horsham, but branch off on the A29 and keep following it, leftwards, to Ockley. Before you the timbered heights of the North Downs loom once more, and you cannot leave Surrey without having scaled Leith Hill and spent time surveying the magnificent pan-

Ockley orama from its summit. Ockley is a collection of tiled Wealden cottages spread on either side of a dead-straight length of the A29, which here follows the course of the Roman Stane Street, the road from Chichester to London. Just past the inn the B2126 turns off left. The first turning right climbs very sharply up to the corniche-type

Leith Hill lane that skirts Leith Hill. Turn left, ignore the lane that drops away to the left, and follow the way around the hill. A short way round the corner there is a car park on the left of the road, and a signpost on the other side pointing up a path to the Tower.

The walk, steadily upward (but not excessively) through the cool tall trees, is about half a mile. At the top there is a clearing, a grassy space, a tall brick-and-red-stone tower (built in 1766, 34 feet high, so that one can be exactly 1,000 feet above sea level), and the finest view in all the South-East.

Before you lies the Weald, still wearing a mantle of green, although if you examine it through glasses you can see the moth-holes eaten by time and the needs of man. More detailed inspection reveals, in fact, a multi-coloured landscape merging distantly into the blue–green belts of woods and hills. Beyond all, standing starkly against the horizon, are the South Downs; directly due south is the tall stand of trees of Chanctonbury Ring, clearly visible, as the Tower behind you is from there. More than any other prospect, certainly than anything seen from the ground, this view gives you an overall impression of the South's natural landscape, for all the works and artefacts merge into and submerge beneath the green blanket. View it at length, consider and remember it, and you may find an answer to those who will say that the South is all roads, houses, and swarming humanity, quite spoiled.

Probably the best way down from Leith Hill is along the lane your car is parked on, through the **Friday Street** deep defiles, the lovely hamlet Friday Street, out to the A25 at Wotton; but if there is time, yet more can be seen of rustic Surrey. First, however, a length of distinctly urban Surrey must be negotiated. Reverse along the way you came, round the southern edge of the hill, and keep on, ignoring all lanes that descend to your right. **Dorking** You arrive in Dorking, and must find your way through to the A24 in the direction of Leatherhead. The road runs through a gap in the Downs made by the mysterious River Mole, which burrows underground in places, and quite soon on your right you will find a large car park *Box Hill* and an ascent on foot up the grassy slopes of Box Hill. It is as popular a picnic spot as ever it was when Jane Austen made her characters in *Emma* go there for that purpose, only to find that the design of a happy day's outing, and the participants' ability to make it so, are two very different things. It is typical of Jane that she does not waste time in describing Box Hill: she is interested only in her characters and their inter-reaction.

Quite near the car park at the base of the hill, on the other side of the road, a lane departs by Westhumble railway station and heads for the hills. Again, the roar of the main road traffic and the bustle of the town recede into the background and are gone: the lane could be in darkest Devon. Trees crowd every hill, the lane is narrow and tortuous, there seem few habitations. You pass a road leading off into the jungle, left, and then there is a lodge-house and a closed gate, and shortly afterwards, when the road has hairpinned up to a higher level, there is a turning *Polesden* left to Polesden Lacey and a return to order and *Lacey* regularity.

A stately, late eighteenth-century house of the Regency period (when George, Prince of Wales, was deputising for his mentally-abstracted father George III), with two wings and a central block with a triangular pediment and a green cupola capping a clock tower, it was given a comprehensive refurbishment in 1906 by its owner, the Hon Mrs Ronald Greville, whose guests to her dinners, lunches, and balls one can still picture, rolling up the gravelled drive in their carriages. The house is open to modern visitors (whether invited or not) every afternoon except Mondays and Fridays.

From the drive to the house turn right into the lane and return the way you came, back down the hairpin and past the lonely lodge-house, until you reach the junction with the other lane. Turn right on it and follow it through its convolutions up to Ranmore Common, then right again along the thickly wooded ridge until you come to a cross-roads. Turn left and descend, with a good deal of care, to the A25. This stretch of country, like that around Leith Hill, is extraordinary, because it exists undisturbed and with all the appearance of distant rural desolation, on the very edge of the extended suburb that reaches from Leatherhead to Lambeth, like the wolf-infested forest just outside a medieval city wall.

Turn right on the A25 and follow it through the attractive, though necessarily noisy, villages of Abinger Hammer and Gomshall. At the junction of the A25 with the A246, cross to the A247 and **Clandon Park** visit Clandon Park, a splendid eighteenth-century mansion built by the Venetian architect Giacomo Leoni for Lord Onslow. Its interior is said to be one of the finest of its period in England. It houses an important collection of Chinese porcelain birds, and it also has the regimental museum of the old Queen's Royal Surreys. Furthermore, even if it is late in the day, it is only a couple of miles back to Guildford.

Windsor

Tourist Information Office
Central Station, tel 52010

Population 31,180

Theatre
Theatre Royal, Thames Street

Cinema
ABC, Thames Street

Places of Interest
Castle
Town Hall
Eton College

Windsor, still dominated by the royal castle, was built for it. For once (unlike Old Romney and Old Alresford), Old Windsor actually existed before the much bigger town called plain Windsor, because when William the Conqueror was looking for a defensible position with which to guard this reach of the Thames, he found a mound in the parish of Clewer, which he swapped for some other manors with the monks of Westminster, and built on it one of his customary wooden strongholds. Old Windsor already existed a little way down-river, and the castle became known as New Windsor, until its importance far outstripped its senior neighbour's.

The castle, built and rebuilt by successive monarchs, offers a history of England on its own: of its military architecture, its kings, its foremost citizens, its traditions. As a royal residence still, with a small garrison of Guardsmen, it attracts visitors by the thousand every day. There is much to see: from Henry VIII's gateway, the last medieval defence work, you might begin with the Horseshoe Cloisters, a perfectly symmetrical semi-circle of timber-and-brick apartments built in the late fifteenth century, to accommodate the chapel clergy. All are occupied, baskets of flowers punctuate the oak supports of their covered passage, brass plates on the doors shine brightly.

The chapel, St George's, replacing an earlier version, represents the highest achievement of all medieval church architecture. The fan-vaulted ceiling, the great west window, the carved wooden choir stalls, and those of the Knights of the Order of the Garter for whom the chapel was built, carry medieval skills to their ultimate perfection. High on the walls outside, the grotesque Queen's Beasts stare for ever out over the town and over the riverside.

The vastly thick Round Tower, at its base, is the oldest visible part, the lower courses perhaps from Henry I's time (he married for the second time, at Windsor), but the State Apartments, despite looking as if the Prince Regent raised them from scratch, are actually a combination of Edward III's, Queen Elizabeth I's, and Charles II's work, and were simply re-arranged and refaced by the extravagant prince after he had at last become George IV. Sumptuous rooms with painted ceilings commissioned by Charles II, state rooms, reception rooms, banqueting rooms, one after another are filled with exquisite furniture and pictures: Holbeins, Rubenses, Van Dycks, Canalettos (a whole roomful) and the Lawrences commissioned by George IV. Queen Victoria's heavy over-decoration overlays much of it, but not so badly as in the Memorial Chapel adjacent to St George's, for her beloved Albert and herself: that has to be seen to be believed.

There is a collection of Leonardo da Vinci's drawings on display in another part of the palace, and in yet another the wonderful doll's house of Queen Mary. From the terraces you can look out over riverside and park listening to the Babel of conversation all around, for all the world is here, and to the incessant roar of airliners rising and descending northward. No matter: they have come, perhaps in the airliners, to see what you are seeing, a unique distillation of the past, rolled into the present ('Is this where the Queen gave that banquet for the President?' the Americans ask) and somehow, imperviously, impressively, permanent.

The Town Hall in Windsor, in addition to several other buildings in the town, such as the perilously leaning Market Cross House, is worth your consideration: when Charles II improved the castle's accommodation the town followed suit. Sir Thomas Fitch designed a new Town Hall, but died before it was finished. Sir Christopher Wren completed it, but his plans were considered unsafe by the councillors, who thought there ought to be columns to hold up the roof. So Wren built columns: but he knew his design was safe enough, so his columns never actually touched the ceiling.

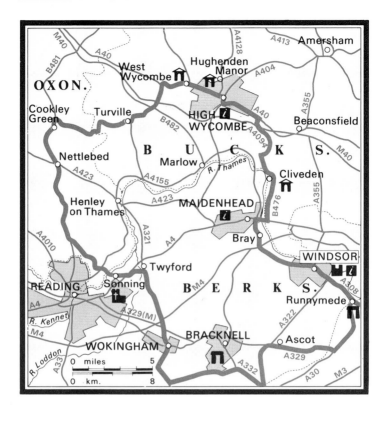

Windsor – Runnymede – Ascot – Wokingham – Sonning – Chiltern Hills – West Wycombe – High Wycombe – Hughenden Manor – Cliveden – Bray – Windsor

Tour length 86 miles

West of London, the landscape in the valley of the River Thames is changeable, and we have to look for the breaks between the lines of houses and towering offices. They are there, and at times during this tour you would not suspect either houses or offices were within fifty miles. At Windsor is a royal residence, within easy reach of the capital; other great houses, as in Surrey and Kent, illustrate the need for responsible public servants to have somewhere quiet and green where they can breathe and think, but not too far from the centre in case of emergency. The beauty of the Thames valley is this balance, the refusal of the natural landscape to be submerged beneath the artificial.

Runnymede The A308 road from Windsor, if followed eastward down-river, leads to Runnymede, a stretch of open grass by the river which has been retained proof against building development. No doubt its appearance today would be quite unrecognisable to King John and his contemporaries, but at least it has not disappeared beneath concrete and asphalt. Much has been said and written about *Magna Carta*, referred to as 'the cornerstone of English liberties', but it was really not much more than a kind of contract between government and power-group. Its existence, as an occasion when a power-group forced a king to moderate his government, was always more significant, as a precedent, than its content. At all events, this level grassy meadow is where the wrangling, the discussion, and the reluctant assent of the king took place, on 15 June 1215.

Back a little way from the pillared entrance to the meadow, the A328 turns off left and takes you away from the crowded riverside road through a

Englefield
Green

surprisingly quiet wooded area to Englefield Green, which still has the look and feel of a village, although surrounded by modern housing. Negotiating the endless roundabouts is difficult, but you must head for the A30 and the direction of Basingstoke, and just past Virginia Water turn off right on the A329. You are skirting the fringe of Windsor Great Park, and notices direct you to Windsor Safari Park, where you may drive through a stretch of English countryside made exotic by the liberation in it of fierce alien beasts, as if those perched on St George's Chapel had come to life and were roaming at large. The A329 also cuts through the thickly wooded park and arrives at Ascot, a small town subservient to the enormous race-course and its buildings. These are accessible to the royal residents of Windsor Castle by a drive across the park, which makes the Ascot meeting so attractive to fashion-conscious society luminaries.

Virginia
Water

Windsor
Safari Park

Ascot

From Ascot turn left on the A332, then sharp right on the A322, turning off it by the first lane to the left. You are travelling all this time since leaving Ascot through dense woodland, which although crossed by paths (and one of them is the Roman road from the cantonal capital *Calleva Atrebatum*, near the modern village of Silchester, to London) is thick and wild, and covers a very large area. In fact it is a surviving part of the great Windsor forest that once stretched from the Thames, south-westward to Bagshot Heath, with a soil similar to that of Hampshire's New Forest. The lane from the A322 cuts straight across the forest, passing on the left the remains of an Iron Age hill-fort called Caesar's Camp (which had nothing to do with Caesar, but certain of our early forefathers assumed that anything they had not constructed or dug themselves must be the work either of Caesar or the Devil: the Roman road just mentioned is known as the Devil's Highway).

Your lane, called Ninemile Ride, crosses the main A3095 road and continues, the woodland thinning out and buildings of various sorts intruding, to the A321. Turn right on this and make for Wokingham.

Wokingham

Like most towns these days, Wokingham has a

one-way system which ushers you away from the town centre. To reach it, coming up from the station, you have to turn right instead of left in Broad Street, which is lined with good old houses and leads to the junction of streets in which, isolated, the Town Hall stands. New shops, in dark-red brick, curving away unobtrusively from this centre, must have been far less controversial when completed than this Town Hall in 1860, for it is a sensation even now, in orange and dark brick, a combination of Gothic, Byzantine, and French château styles.

The A321, if followed out of Wokingham, leaves the forest for the flat plains of the Rivers Kennet and Loddon, as they meander towards the Thames. It crosses two motorways (the A329M **Twyford** and the M4) and takes you to Twyford, where you turn left on the A3032, then at Charvil cross over the A4 to the B478 and go down to the Thames at Sonning.

Sonning   The only trouble with Sonning is that parking places are not easy to come by, but if you can find some corner (perhaps as a patron of the *Bull Inn*) the village is worth your regard. Its houses are grouped around a network of narrow streets and passages, and include a number of timbered cottages, uncharacteristically painted white with blackened timber, and some graceful brick houses of the seventeenth and eighteenth centuries. The humped brick bridge crosses the river (which needs to be crossed several more times, because like the Test, but on a larger scale, it has many streams) and the Thames riverside scene is before you. Along its whole length from Windsor to Oxford, combining the eternal fascination of gliding, shining smooth water with the grace of waterside willows and the charm of mellowed brick-and-tile houses, bright with flowers, pleasure-boats moored at the banks, people taking their ease, it has the power to glue the visitor to the spot in admiring contemplation.

Bridges cross the other branches of the river, and for the first time in these tours of South-East England, you are north of its principal river. The lane crosses the A4155 road and starts to climb **Dunsden** into the first agricultural country of the day, **Green** forking left at the pretty hamlet Dunsden Green.

The lane is narrow, the landscape totally rustic: the change from the preceding conditions astonishing in so short a distance. You are climbing gradually into the Chiltern Hills.

The lane meets the B481 road, on the corner of which is a good inn called the *Bird in Hand*, and the road will carry you through the unexciting housing of Sonning Common, the village Rotherfield Peppard, and undulating farmland, fairly thickly wooded. At **Nettlebed** it crosses the A423 and at Cookley Green it turns right on the B480, a lane which runs along a surprising valley called Pishill Bottom, flanked by ridges piled high with the loveliest of beech-woods, reminiscent of Selborne Hanger. Houses and even farmsteads are infrequent, but still clearer introduction to Chiltern rural solitude is at hand. At the end of the valley a lane goes off left, signposted Turville, and if you follow this as it winds deeply into the hills and woods, taking a right fork at **Turville Heath** and making for Fingest, encountering few other road-users and fewer inhabitants, you may form the impression that no one has ever bothered to settle north of the Thames.

Since crossing the river you have so far been in Oxfordshire. At Balham's Farm, just after turning off the Pishill Bottom lane, you cross the border into Buckinghamshire. This has little effect on the scenery: the Chilterns are like the North Downs, in that the dense woods and the deep valleys determine the nature of settlement. Neither is easy to cultivate or build on, and communication can only be by permission of the elements. Deep snow or heavy rain renders the lanes impassable in no time.

The spell woven by these enchanted hills is broken after **Fingest** because you encounter first some houses, then cross the B482, then pass under the M40 motorway, and at last meet the main A40 road. Turn right on it, past an inn called the *Dashwood Arms*, and soon on your left you will see a wooded hill with a golden cupola protruding from the topmost trees. This is **West Wycombe**, and on the roadside a large signboard invites you to partake of the pleasures in a Garden Centre, a Mausoleum, the Church of St

Windsor

Lawrence, a Motor Museum, and the Hell-Fire Caves in the hill. The Hell-Fire Club consisted of a group of wealthy layabouts, led by Sir Francis Dashwood, who in the mid-eighteenth century acquired a scurrilous reputation for drunken and disorderly conduct. Sir Francis built a stately and tasteful house, off the road opposite the hill, in the classical Palladian style (although not a rotunda like Mereworth).

High Wycombe The A40 road into High Wycombe is unfortunately unappealing, and only recommended because in the town you can turn left on the A4128, and after a mile or two you come to **Hughenden Manor** Hughenden Manor. Although it is not a particularly beautiful house, built in the eighteenth century in dark red brick, it was bought in 1847 by Benjamin Disraeli, MP, who subsequently became one of Britain's most eminent Prime Ministers. As Chartwell with Churchill, Hughenden is kept as Disraeli left it, full of pictures, souvenirs, and accumulated gifts, all recalling his life and occupation, with his wife, of the house. Some of the rooms are furnished in the style of the period (which means they are dark and heavily over-ornamented) and for anyone interested in the personalities of Victorian politics, including the Queen herself who favoured Disraeli as a friend, Hughenden has a great deal to offer. The house itself is well-proportioned and the garden represents that haven of cool green peace that any overworked statesman must have been glad of, when he had time to relax.

Returning to High Wycombe and escaping from it left along the A40, which follows the course of the small River Wye, you can leave it by turning right on the A4094, which passes under the M40 and dives into a steep-sided valley in the hills, made by the Wye's course to the Thames. At Cores End you turn off left on the B476, which skirts the steep hills above the Thames. Between the road and the river, set in a wonderful park, is **Cliveden** a mid-nineteenth-century house called Cliveden, once the home of our first lady MP, Nancy, Lady Astor. The beauty of the grounds and gardens, with delightful walks through the trees and views of the river, exceeds that of the house.

The B476, keeping discreetly to the trees so that

you can hardly see the river, meets the main A4 road. Turn right and cross the river by Maidenhead bridge, which is just upstream from Brunel's railway bridge, whose arches, at 128 feet each, were at the time the biggest-ever span in brick. After crossing the river, turn left on the B3028: it not only points you back in the direction of Windsor, but takes you to the lovely riverside village of Bray.

Bray

There is plenty to see in Bray. There are timber-framed cottages, the oldest of which is the *Crown* inn, which may have two projecting brick wings but whose centre derives from a fourteenth-century hall-house. There are eighteenth-century brick houses, such as Chantry House by the churchyard and the Jesus Hospital, founded in 1627 according to the will of one William Goddard, whose statue is in a niche over the gatehouse. There is also Lych Cottage, a timber-and-brick cottage of the fifteenth century under which you pass to enter the churchyard, and there is the church itself. On its far side there is a little flint chantry chapel, used as a school at one time. The big church has its original Perpendicular tower but was heavily 'restored' in 1859. One rather dubious claim to fame is that its incumbent from 1522 to 1565 was the morally unscrupulous Vicar of Bray, Simon Symonds or Alleyn. So determined was he to cling to his lucrative living that he weathered all the theological vicissitudes of the period, through Henry VIII's refutation of the Pope, the Protestant Reformation, the return of Catholicism under Queen Mary I, and the establishment of the Church of England by Elizabeth I, simply by changing his doctrine to suit them all. A popular song of about 1720 altered the period to one more recent, applying the same unprincipled and devious apostasies to the religious policies of the High Church Stuarts and the Protestant German Georges. But the proclamation remains the same, 'That whatsoever King shall reign, I'll still be the Vicar of Bray, Sir.'

Continuing on the B3028 you meet the A308 close by the overpassing M4, and it is only 5 miles altogether back to Windsor.

Bedford

Tourist Information Office
St Paul's Square, tel 67422

Population 69,170

Theatre
Civic Theatre, Horn Lane

Cinema
Granada, St Peter's Street

Museum
Bunyan Collection

Places of Interest
Bridge and riverside
Cecil Higgins Art Collection

The county town of Bedford cannot claim to be one of the most beautiful, nor the most interesting of English shire towns. Its most pleasing feature is the River Ouse, which flows through it, the main part of the town being on its northern bank. Its chief claim to fame is that John Bunyan, the sturdy religious writer of the seventeenth century, was born at Elstow nearby and lived in Bedford most of his life.

There are plenty of good shops, banks, and inns in Bedford, and one of the most comfortable of hotels (*De Parys Hotel*, in De Parys Avenue). Despite its modest claim to tourists' attention, it is an excellent centre for the exploration of the valley of the Great Ouse, in the East Midlands.

Bedford – Elstow – Houghton House – Woburn Abbey – Ampthill – Sandy – St Neots – Godmanchester – St Ives – Huntingdon – Kimbolton – Bedford

Tour length 92 miles

One of the most noticeable features, to a tourist, of East Anglia, is that distances appear to be much greater between the things he wants to visit. This tour merely explores the interesting towns, villages, and houses in a section of the valley of the River Ouse (known as the Great Ouse) and yet to do so is obliged to cover nearly twice the distance of a comparable tour in, say, Kent. With the distance comes an appropriate feeling of space, for although the region is certainly not woodless, there are no great forests, and one has not the impression of being entirely hemmed in and lost among the darkening trees: there is always light and air, fresh and breezy.

Elstow John Bunyan, whose *Pilgrim's Progress* is in the first rank of religious allegory, was born and lived at Elstow, which is only a mile or so out of Bedford on the A6. The main road splits it in two, a serious detriment to any village, and great efforts have been made to remedy the fission by restoring old cottages and making a small estate of new cottages in harmony with the old. On the left of the road, from Bedford, there is a long row of timbered cottages of the sixteenth century, in excellent repair and grafted on to the sympathetic new additions. Across the road there is a large green on which stands the Moot Hall, also of the sixteenth century, a two-storey building with a timber frame, its upright studding in-filled with brick, with a tiled roof. It houses a John Bunyan museum.

The parish church nearby is the remnant of Elstow Abbey, a former Benedictine nunnery, whose church was in part used by the parish before the Dissolution and continued after it; its slow development can be traced in the Norman eastern end giving way to Early English work in the western bays, although all is overlain by the

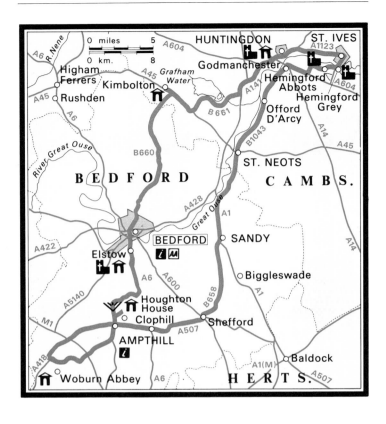

restoration in 1880. Unusually, it has a detached bell-tower of the late fourteenth century. On the far side of the church are the remains of the great house which replaced the conventual buildings (no doubt using the same material).

Bunyan's career and reputation are shared between Elstow and Bedford, because although he lived much of his life in Elstow, the more important part, connected with his conversion, preaching, imprisonment, and writing, was centred on Bedford. His spell in prison, which lasted twelve years altogether, could have been much shorter or even non-existent, but Bunyan was one of those uncompromising characters who will accept no mitigation of his belief in the freedom to say and do what he thinks is right. He owed much to his two wives: his first was responsible for his reform from hard-swearing roisterer to evangelical proselyte, and the second supported him heroically throughout his prison term and for the rest of his life. His formal education had been minimal, so that the vigour of his literary style and the prolificacy of his output can be reckoned almost miraculous.

Houghton Conquest

After two more miles of the A6 a turning right takes you to Houghton Conquest, a quiet village in the shadow of a looming forest of chimneys belonging to adjacent brick-fields. The landscape so far has been uniformly level and placidly arable and pastoral, but after turning left on the A418 you begin to climb a hill out of the wide vale on the way to Ampthill. At the top there is a

Houghton House

modest lane signposted to Houghton House: long and narrow, it leads to a spur of the hills and a splendid ruin. There is a small car park, and a $\frac{1}{4}$-mile walk farther along the track. The ruin, of a brick-built Jacobean mansion, stands gaunt against the sky, its empty window-frames like staring skull's eyes.

Mary, Countess of Pembroke, the brother of Sir Philip Sidney of Penshurst Place, was not left at all well off by her husband the earl when he died in 1601. She was only 40, and when presented at Court earned the favour of James I and his queen. James granted her the royal manor of Houghton, and here she built this fine mansion, where she entertained the king and queen in

1621. She was intelligent and gifted, like her brother, and with him undertook a complete translation of the Psalms, most of which was her work. The house is said to have been embellished by Inigo Jones, because the added Renaissance Italianate porches and loggias have his touch. The result was a graceful, elegant, compact house, made more handsome still by its position, on the spur of the hills commanding a staggering expanse of landscape.

The house and estate were eventually bought by the Duke of Bedford in the late eighteenth century. Finding it redundant he dismantled it in 1794, although it was never demolished. Perhaps the present Duke may have regretted his ancestor's philistinism, since, alone and silent on its windy promontory, the house has grace and beauty still.

Back on the road and into Ampthill (to which we shall return) you turn right with the A418 for **Woburn** Woburn, where you can visit the celebrated Woburn Abbey, seat of the Duke of Bedford (although it is at present occupied and administered by his son the Marquess of Tavistock). Like Windsor, it has a Safari Park as a separate entity for those who like looking at lions through their windscreens, but the chief attraction is the great house itself, whose origins lie in the Cistercian abbey it replaced, but whose major construction in Charles I's time is disguised by Henry Flitcroft's classical central block and wings of the 1750s. The Russell family, first as earls, then dukes of Bedford, have owned it since the Dissolution, and their accumulation of paintings and art treasures over the years (including 22 Canalettos of Venice) makes it an art museum on its own. The park is filled with varieties of deer and cattle, and may be visited independently of the house.

If you have not stayed all day here, there is plenty more for you to do and see. From the park you can reach the lane past Eversholt to **Ampthill** Steppingley and back to Ampthill, which is a delightful little hill-top town on a cross-roads, filled with cottages in the local Bedfordshire style, timber-framed, brick in-filled, and usually thatched. These cottages mingle with ivy-clad

Georgian town-houses, to give a wholly pleasing impression. Turn right in Ampthill on the A507 *Shefford* through Clophill to Shefford, left on the A600 and quickly right on the B658 to Sandy.

You have now descended from the hills into the Ouse basin, an immense, wide-open, light and breezy plain, with arable fields stretching into the distance on either hand, distantly lined with woods. The B658 takes you away from the traffic-filled A roads (but even they are not quite so hectic as those farther south) and gives you a gentle introduction to the East Anglian scene.

Sandy   Bypassing Sandy on the old A1, you can leave it fairly quickly by taking the right turn offered by *Tempsford* the B1043 beyond Tempsford. Here you are nearer the Ouse itself and can follow its willows through St Neots, Great Paxton, Offord D'Arcy, and Offord Cluny, to Godmanchester. The small *St Neots* country town of St Neots and the riverside villages are full of the kind of thatched cottages seen in Ampthill and the atmosphere of stout country independence, precisely the kind of places that supplied Oliver Cromwell with his sturdy troopers 'with the root of the matter in them', who would fight, like himself and like Bunyan, for what they believed was right. As you *Godmanchester* approach Godmanchester you may see on your right a big, plain, no-nonsense brick house of the eighteenth century which may well be contrasted with the Prince Regent's flippant frills or Dashwood's fashionable extravagance.

At Godmanchester turn right on the A604 for a short spell, then take the first turning left, *Hemingford* towards the river, and visit Hemingford Abbots. *Abbots* A cluster of little thatched brick-and-timber cottages around a tall-spired Perpendicular church, a tiny tree-shaded square with a very good inn (also thatched), the sweet scent of new-mown grass and flowers from the gardens, and birdsong in the quiet air, could keep you wandering contentedly about all day. Its neighbour *Hemingford* Hemingford Grey is larger and busier, but on the *Grey* river-bank you can forget the noise and the lorries and simply watch the shining, placid river gliding by the willows, little boys fishing, and small boats pottering about. One of the ubiquitous thatched cottages is on the bank, the church tower rises behind others, and all is sweet harmony.

St Ives Nearby St Ives, also straddling the river, is bigger still, a bustling small town, with narrow crowded streets and a market place (in full spate on Mondays) which in spirit cannot have changed much since Cromwell's time. A vigorous statue of that resolute character overlooks the chaffering and dealing, because he was for some time a citizen of St Ives.

Since it is time now to head back up-river, turn left from St Ives on to the A1123. Quite **Huntingdon** soon you are in Huntingdon, where there is a large car park behind a modern shopping precinct. The two Hemingford villages, St Ives, Godmanchester, and Huntingdon are all clustered around a five-mile stretch of the river, which testifies to the fertility of the immediate hinterland and to the former commercial faculty of the river for transport. This is Cromwell country, and you cannot be in Huntingdon for long without reference to its most famous son. He was born here, in 1599, went to school here, and lived here until 1630, when he moved to St Ives. The way through the shopping precinct brings you into the High Street. Turn right, and a short way along, on the right, you come to a patched-up Norman chapel which used to be the school Cromwell attended, and now houses a small museum. Continuing along the High Street, near its end you will see Cromwell House, with his coat-of-arms over the door to prove it. Here he was born, although if its apparently eighteenth-century style is a guide, the house was subsequently refaced, if not rebuilt.

Huntingdon has a substantial ration of good old houses, including a big square Town Hall with the obligatory clock, and some intriguing little by-ways.

Cromwell, although himself not particularly well-off, was at least well-connected, and on the A604 road going towards Kettering there is a **Hinchingbrooke** sumptuous mansion built in the sixteenth cen-
House tury by an ancestor.

Oliver Cromwell in fact owes his name to the high and mighty Thomas Cromwell, First Secretary and Vicegerent to King Henry VIII, hammer of the monks. This potentate, having lined his pocket most sedulously, never married and had no issue, so willed his rich estate to his sister's children. This lady having married a Welshman called Morgan Williams, and Oliver being her great-great-grandson, his name should have been Williams, but Thomas Cromwell stipulated that his sister's children should change their name to Cromwell in order to inherit his wealth. Her grandson, Sir Henry Cromwell, built this magnificent palace on the site of the nunnery of Hinchingbrooke, with much former monastic land to supply him, but his son (Oliver's uncle) spent his wealth and sold out to yet another branch of the Montagu family.

From Hinchingbrooke House, which you can only admire from without, continue along the A604, then turn left on the A141 and left again for a short dash along the A1. Take the first right from this busy main road, on the B661 to Grafham Water: it is a big reservoir made by damming a tributary to the Ouse. On a sunny day it is a delight to walk along the long grassy stretch by its side. There are water-birds to watch, fish to catch if you are so inclined, and the freedom to sniff the air and stretch your legs.

Grafham Water

This B661 road meets the A45, and if you turn right, in a short while you can reach the village of Kimbolton, which is rather overshadowed by the huge gateway (like Petworth in Sussex) of Kimbolton Castle. In its present state this is not a castle, but like Mereworth is an eighteenth-century replacement for one, a massive, grey, classically-proportioned mansion, whose State Rooms are open for inspection on Sunday afternoons. Kimbolton itself is a pleasant little place, with a wide street containing some interesting inns and houses. If you return along the A45 and take the B660 on the right, you can then make your way back to Bedford.

Kimbolton

Cambridge

Tourist Information Office
4 Benedict Street, tel 58977

Population 98,519

Theatre
Cambridge Arts Theatre, Peas Hill

Cinemas
ABC, 1 and 2, St Andrew's Street
ADC, Park Street
Arts Cinema, Market Passage
Victoria, 1 and 2, Market Hill

Museums
Fitzwilliam Museum, Trumpington Street
Folk Museum, Northampton Street
Museum of of Archaeology and Anthropology, Downing Street
Museum of Geology, Downing Street
Museum of Zoology, Downing Street
Museum of Classical Archaeology, Peterhouse
Kettles Yard, Paintings and Sculptures, Northampton Street
Whipple Museum of Science, Free School Lane

Places of Interest

St John's Gatehouse

Great Court and fountain, Trinity

King's College Chapel

The Backs

Botanic Gardens

Great St Mary's Church

Holy Sepulchre Church

Various other colleges

As you can see from the above information, Cambridge really deserves a week or more to itself, there is so much to see and appreciate. For an appetiser, I can recommend walking along King's Parade on a summer evening when the sky is clear and the setting sun has left tints of pink and lilac and violet, gold and orange, before which the towers and pinnacles of the colleges are silhouetted in black velvet. Lamps glow yellow in the courtyards and quadrangles, the sound of music drifts from the lit halls and you become aware of the peculiar magic imparted by superbly fashioned and well-loved buildings, filled with lively activity. The effect, in the half-light, is sensationally exciting.

Daylight produces no disenchantment, only allowing you to see more clearly the Perpendicular splendour of King's College Chapel, the symmetrical Renaissance grace of Clare, the fussy grandeur of St John's gatehouse. At the end of St John's Street and across Sidney Street, look at the church of the Holy

Sepulchre, which is perfectly circular. It owes its shape and construction to returning First Crusaders, who wanted a tiny replica of the great Temple in Jerusalem which they had seized from the Turks. Its mixture of Byzantine with Norman Romanesque, with a lovely double-arched triforium gallery, is offset by the added chancel and north aisle. The latter has a carved oak ceiling from the fourteenth century, the ceiling of the chancel and south aisle are later copies. The church was first built in about 1130.

Walk down Sidney Street and peep into the quadrangles of Sidney Sussex or Christ's Colleges. They have smooth green lawns, ancient medieval halls, and lodges gay with flowers, and the prevalent atmosphere of orderly serenity, like a cathedral precinct's, contrasts startingly with the noisy clamour of the street a few feet away. There have been colleges of teachers in Cambridge since the thirteenth century, and students have always flocked around them. So the college buildings have gradually arisen, added to as the need for academic knowledge has intensified. The colleges and their erudite teachers, representing the poised and balanced harmonious beauty of Apollo; the students and the townspeople, vital and vigorous, passionate with the disturbing sensuality of Dionysus: all the compulsions and contradictions of the human race can be sensed in the concentrated intensity of a university town.

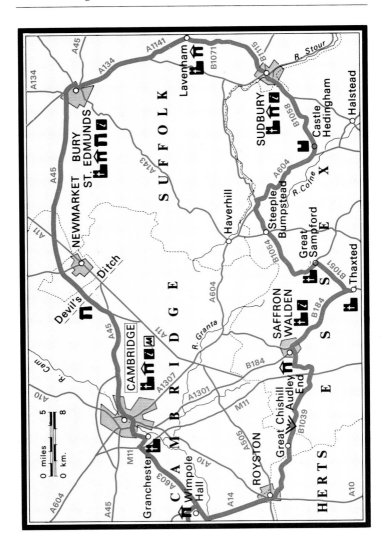

Cambridge – Grantchester – Wimpole Hall – Saffron Walden – Thaxted – Castle Hedingham – Sudbury – Lavenham – Bury St Edmunds – Cambridge

Tour length 110 miles

The countryside around Cambridge is rich in interest, but East Anglian distances mean that even in a tour of this length not all the attractions can be visited. Ideally, three or four tours should be arranged, one especially to include the Cathedral of Ely, which for reasons of distance and time has had to be omitted. In this verdant rolling landscape, the evidence of past wealth is apparent: there are the great houses, the stoutly-built little towns, the remains of one of England's greatest monasteries. This is wool country; yet when you look about today, few sheep can be seen, for the land taken from the plough in the Middle Ages and given to sheep has now gone back to the plough.

Grantchester Rupert Brooke made us all aware of Grantchester, and for his sake, and for our own curiosity's, it is easy to go there: out of Cambridge on the A603 towards Sandy and turning off it left, within a mile. At once the suburban houses, of which there are few on this side of the town anyway, give place to open farmland, and before long you reach the T of lanes around which the village clusters. Brooke, of course, fortunately for him knew nothing of the M11 motorway which now passes within yards, and can hardly permit much of the 'peace and holy quiet there' that he so admires. Nor does the church clock stand at ten to three, if it ever did other than at that time twice a day, because it is going and right. But it must be admitted that Brooke's disparaging rhymes about people from the rest of the entire neighbourhood keep coming to mind: 'For Cambridge people rarely smile . . .' Some do.

Grantchester's cottages are pretty, mostly thatched, as are many in other villages, uncommemorated in verse but farther removed from the unholy din of a motorway. Turn right at

Grantchester's T-junction and find the A603: it flies over the motorway and makes off in the direction of the A14 as purposefully as when the Romans built both of them. Just before the A14, called Ermine Street, is reached however, a lane **Wimpole Hall** to the right signposted to Wimpole Hall could be followed, for Wimpole Hall is a splendid early Georgian house, with the classical central block and two projecting wings. A large Venetian window beneath a triangular pediment occupies the centre over the door, at the head of a series of balustraded steps. A massive stable block nearby is dated 1851. The house opens at 2 pm, and if you are there earlier you can stand in solitude, contemplating the smooth park grass, the grand old trees, and the faint ethereal suggestion of its orderly eighteenth-century life: gardeners, stable-men with the horses, maids and footmen busy about the house, boys polishing harness. The ghosts vanish when the modern visitors arrive and the house opens.

Royston Returning to the last remaining yards of the A603, go to the A14 and follow it left to Royston, making sure that you go to the town centre, because there is a large and confusing round-about outside the town. Beyond Royston the old Ermine Street continues as the A10, and from it while still in the town the B1039 leads off left to Saffron Walden. As a contrast to the undeviating Ermine Street, this road was clearly marked out by Chesterton's 'rolling English drunkard'. It goes through mildly hilly country whose modest heights afford fine views of the surrounding landscape. Woods are few, and so are villages: the fields that once were as white-studded with sheep as Romney Marsh are now arable and corn-bearing. One curiosity, apart from the village names (Great Chishill, Chrishall, Wendens Ambo), is that you keep dodging in and out between the counties of Cambridgeshire and Essex. These anomalies in county boundaries, if they do not follow the serpentine course of some river, are often the result of some long-forgotten medieval manor limits. Much that appears in-explicably obtuse in English affairs has a reason, but often it is very far removed from present needs and conditions.

The B1039 meets the B1383. If you turn left on it, then right on a lane signposted Audley End, you may visit a splendid early seventeenth-century Jacobean mansion, in sumptuous parkland carefully landscaped with lakes, a Roman temple, a Greek temple, and a column (and a golf course). **Audley End** is vast, and was renovated in the eighteenth century with exquisite taste by Adam. All his work has recently been refreshed so that the colours and proportions have been regained. The Neville family, Lords Braybrooke, long owned and occupied the house, and the rooms are full of portraits of their numerous and well-known relations and connections. Many of these, with some other fine paintings and superb furniture, came to the Nevilles when one of them married a daughter of Lord Cornwallis in the late eighteenth century. If you can merge the images in this living, beautifully appointed palace, with the ghosts outside Wimpole Hall (if you sensed them), you may be able to slip back in your mind two hundred years and picture that age of contrasts.

Saffron Walden shows in its wide sloping street where its money came from: the solid houses, the big Perpendicular church of the fifteenth century seem to shout Wool Trade. On the Cambridge road out, there is a marvellous old inn called the *Eight Bells*, where you will be well-fed, if you can avoid concussion from its low-timbered ceiling.

From Saffron Walden, the B184 will take you to **Thaxted**, the second of the tour's three examples of wool-fattened East Anglian towns. It is smaller, but more complete, again on a slope, again with the most magnificent of all parish churches in the height of the Perpendicular style, whose tall-steepled exterior is fully matched by the glories inside. The church is at the top of the hill. Lower down, where the High Street broadens, stands a tall timbered Market Hall, with an arcaded lower storey and a little lock-up, and a slightly later house tucked in behind it. There is nothing of the ghost-town about Thaxted, the houses are in good order, and the streets full of shops. Good fertile farmland will go on supplying wealth, if properly husbanded, to any generation.

Return up the hill past the church, and if you

now turn right on the B1051 you can enjoy a long drive in this deeply rural and intensely cultivated country, gently up and down its mild vales, seeing few villages, savouring the rich smells from corn, soil, and hedgerows, wafting on **Great** the bright air. Turn left at Great Sampford, then **Sampford** fork right to the B1054, through Hempstead and Steeple Bumpstead until the road meets the A604. Follow this right through Ridgewell and Great Yeldham to Castle Hedingham.

A compact and attractive village of brick, timber, and thatch cottages clusters on a hillside beneath a commanding height, crowned elusively (since it is discreetly curtained by tall trees) with **Castle** a mighty Norman castle keep: Castle **Hedingham** Hedingham. Built and held for generations by the family de Vere, earls of Oxford, the keep arose in about 1100. It is still over 100 feet high, a tall, grey, forbidding mass, approached by a long and circuitous drive and a brick bridge across its deep dry ditch. Far less well-known than the Tower of London or Rochester, this is nevertheless one of the best preserved early Norman keeps, guarding the interior from possible access along the valley of the River Colne.

From the castle it is easy to find the B1058 road to Sudbury, to reach which you cross the River Stour, the boundary at this point with Suffolk. In its lower reaches, the Stour provided John Constable with his famous series of subjects, which has brought it much attention, as we shall see. You may have noticed that river names tend to be duplicated throughout the country: we have encountered two Rothers, two Ouses (three if you count Little Ouse and Great Ouse separately), and two Stours. Many river names are of very early, Celtic origin, simply taken over by the Anglo-Saxon settlers. Stour is thought to derive from a Celtic word meaning strong, or forceful, and Ouse is one of many words for water. In the Gaelic form of Celtic the word *uisge* means water (*uisge beatha* is the water of life, whisky) and rivers called Ouse, Usk, Axe, Exe, and Esk appear to be derivations of the same word.

Sudbury Sudbury has a number of timbered houses of the sixteenth and seventeenth centuries and two good medieval churches, one of which, St Gregory's, was rebuilt in the late fourteenth century by Archbishop Simon of Sudbury, who also rebuilt Canterbury's city walls and gateways, and was an unfortunate victim of the Peasants' Revolt. Members of the more violent section of the peasants beheaded him, and some thoughtful person must have saved the fallen head, because his skull is preserved in St Gregory's vestry. Another East Anglian painter, Thomas Gainsborough, was born in a house in Sudbury in 1727, a sixteenth-century building refaced in the Georgian style, like so many town houses. His house is now, appropriately enough, an art centre.

From Sudbury take the B1115 in the direction of Stowmarket, then fork left on the B1071 to **Lavenham** Lavenham. By far the best of the wool-towns, Lavenham is worth exploring at length, on foot. The tall-towered fifteenth-century Perpendicular church stands at the top of the curving, sloping High Street, whose houses, nearly all built during the hundred years between 1450 and 1550, front directly on the pavements. East of the High Street, behind the *Swan Hotel*, stands Corpus Christi Guildhall in the Market Square, built in 1520. Cloth-weaving is what founded this town's fortune, good stout woollen cloth from the local wool, in such international demand that the weavers enjoyed a long period of unparalleled prosperity. Every one of these houses is a marvel, especially when you consider that, the chief material being wood, and the normal artificial lighting until fifty years ago lamps and candles, the odds on the whole lot burning down must have been very long.

Lavenham stands on the junction of the B1071 with the A1141, which can now be followed in the direction of Bury St Edmunds. Places are well spaced out in East Anglia, the countryside is devoted to broad acres of corn, with occasional herds of cattle but not many sheep these days. The hills are inconsiderable, but that does not prevent the roads from meandering about all over the place, Z-bends following fast one upon another. If roads are straight in East Anglia, it is usually because they were engineered in Roman times. They were therefore in existence when the Anglo-Saxons came and settled, and looked for land boundaries. Other boundaries were harder to fix, and tracks between manors were obliged to dodge fastidiously between the great open fields. These tracks having supplied the only feasible communications, they continued in their snake-like form long after the original manor-boundaries had fallen into disuse, with successive enclosures of land from the Middle Ages to the eighteenth century.

Bury St Edmunds Bury St Edmunds is a town all on a hillside, leading down to the remains of the mighty abbey that waxed fat on the same means as all Suffolk. Not a great deal is left of the abbey (also known as St Edmundsbury), which was the most important in England. In its heyday its colossal Romanesque church, over 500 feet long, was one of the biggest in Europe, with a resplendent west front. Two gateways remain, one Norman, high and handsome, the other fourteenth-century, much more ornate. Between them is the Cathedral Church of St James, founded after the Dissolution and restored in the nineteenth century.

Opposite the abbey walls in Angel Hill is the ivy-covered *Angel Hotel*, a four-storey Georgian coaching inn, and Angel Corner, a Queen Anne house with a collection of clocks and watches on display. The rising streets, full of houses worthy of attention, lead to the Market Square, with porticoed and colonnaded Town Hall and Corn Exchange, and the ancient Guildhall. The size of the Abbey, the obvious continuation of prosperity in the town after the sale of raw or woven wool had declined, and the splendour of these last public buildings give a fair indication of the inherent wealth to be derived from the Suffolk countryside.

Much time could be spent in Bury St Edmunds, because there is much in the old streets and the stone antiquities of this near-vanished abbey that deserves more prolonged exploration, but the tour has come a long way and there is still a fair distance back to Cambridge.

The most direct way back is on the A45, which by-passes Newmarket and its race-course, but it still cuts across the so-called Devil's Ditch, an East Anglian version of Offa's Dyke: that is, a defence-work, probably dug to protect the East Angles from attack either by Britons or rival groups of invaders, fairly early in the Anglo-Saxon period (fifth to sixth century). It runs at right angles to the Roman road, now the A11, as if the defenders were expecting an attack to come along it, from either direction.

St Johns College

Aldeburgh

Tourist Information Office
Borough Offices, Victoria Road, tel 2971

Population 2,970

Cinema
Aldeburgh Cinema, High Street

Museum
Moot Hall

Places of Interest
Moot Hall
Customs House

The coast of East Anglia is as changeable as that of Kent. Some ports, such as Great Yarmouth and Harwich, have managed to maintain their maritime function. Others, like Dunwich, have been swept away into the sea by the eroding winds and storms, and others still, like Aldeburgh, have been left without a port, because the same winds and tides have piled up shingle along the mouth of a river, blocking its entrance. Thus Aldeburgh, once a port with a safe haven in the River Alde, lost its living and had to rely on fish from the sea.

Now it prospers again, partly because of its own fresh and charming character and the feeling it gives to visitors of being remote from everywhere, and partly because of its new fame as a centre for live music of a high order. Since 1948, at the instigation of its most celebrated late resident, Sir Benjamin Britten, it has had an annual festival, based on the concert hall fashioned out of old malthouses at Snape, not far away. Britten's music and operas themselves have featured Aldeburgh and its district, and it is not difficult, as you walk along the beach, seeing the town's fishing-boats still drawn up ready for another night's work, to the old Moot Hall, to understand his fascination with the place.

Houses, some very old, some more recent, and a few hotels, such as the big *White Lion*, line the sea-front road, facing the sea. Between them and the beach the Moot Hall stands as it has since the sixteenth century. Like Elstow's, it is a timber-framed building gabled at each end, with decorated barge-boards on the northern end, close-studded upright timbers and brick in-filling between them. It is on two storeys, and a wooden staircase leads outside (on the landward side) to the first floor. Intended, as its name implies, for meetings of the townspeople, it still houses (in addition to a museum) the office of the Town Clerk and is still used for council meetings.

At the opposite end of the beach is the spacious and comfortable *Brudenell Hotel*, from which you can see the sea, because it is right in front of it, and the silvery reaches of the River Alde as it winds its tantalising way alongside the sea-shore. Behind the sea-front houses and hotels the High Street runs laterally, wide and handsome, and the late medieval church stands up on the rise behind the town, by the road leading inland to the heathy wilderness separating the coast from the fertile hinterland. For the sporting, there is a golf course in this wilderness, and another a little way along the coast at Thorpeness, and of course there is plenty of sailing and fishing. With bird-watching and music too, there is much to attract the visitors to make up for the loss of its ship-sheltering haven.

Moot Hall, Aldeburgh

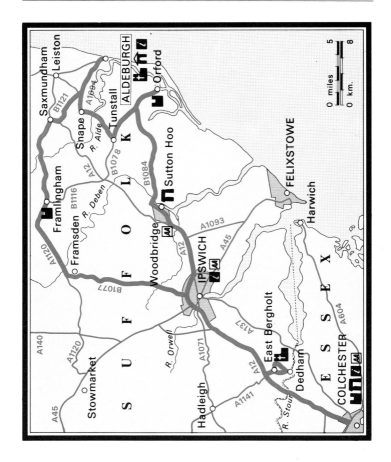

Aldeburgh – Snape – Orford – Woodbridge – Colchester – East Bergholt – Flatford – Framlingham – Aldeburgh

Tour length 98 miles

A round tour of so indented a coastline being somewhat difficult to envisage, this is more in the nature of an excursion from Aldeburgh to some of the interesting places within reach. In the northern section of the shore-line, around Aldeburgh, there is a wide sandy stretch of forest land, very thinly populated. Farther south, the broad, flat estuaries enable the sea to stretch its fingers into Essex and offer sites for seaports and opportunities for fishing for the industrious and boating for the pleasure-seeking. Such a coastline, offering as it has for centuries similar invitations (but in reverse) to sea-borne invaders, needs defence, and the tour includes three castles.

Snape

The A1094 road, which connects Aldeburgh with the rest of the world, passes first over the heathery moor, with the land-locked Alde haven to the left, then meets the B1069. If you turn along this you will come quickly to Snape, and having emerged on the far side of the quiet village you will then cross a bridge over the Alde. On your left is a long row of functional buildings, several capped with pyramidic cowls. There is also an inn. The foremost range of buildings include some in current commercial use, the remainder in the rear are part of the complex that has evolved around the Maltings Concert Hall. One of the blocks in this extensive brick-built malting works, at the rear of the Hall, is the Britten–Pears School of Music, and strains of piano, violin, or voice issuing from it show that business is good. There are also adjuncts such as a shop and a wine-bar, and moored to the quayside at the bridge there is a sailing barge on show. The breeze, channelled along the Alde flats from the sea, is fresh and vigorous, gulls squeal petulantly around your head, and a place farther removed from the probability of producing serious music would be hard to imagine. Yet, as at

Glyndebourne, another isolated oasis of the musical world, performers come from all over the world to play here.

Pursuing your course along the B1069 to Tunstall, you turn left on the B1078 and return to Suffolk's version of the New Forest. As in that part of Hampshire, the acid sandy soil will support few crops but plenty of trees, bracken, gorse, and heather. Tunstall Forest consists mainly of Forestry Commission conifers. The road joins the B1084 and drops down to Orford.

Aldeburgh and Orford once shared importance as ports on the River Alde, which issued into the sea nearby (today it does so another 5 miles farther south, at Hollesley Bay), and in the twelfth century, when King Stephen's mildness, coupled with the challenge to his tenure of the throne by his cousin Matilda, weakened royal authority, both towns were under the control of Hugh Bigod, Earl of Norfolk. Matilda's son succeeded to the throne as Henry II in 1154, and set about restoring order. In 1157 he confiscated all the earl's castles, only permitting him, years later in 1165, to receive back Framlingham and Bungay for a fine of £1,000. But by then Henry had begun to build a new castle of his own, between Framlingham and the sea at Orford, of so new and strong a design that Bigod never dared to attack it.

Standing on the very edge of the promontory above the creek that led to the Alde and the sea, Orford Castle has a keep and a curtain wall: that was nothing uncommon, they all did. Orford's keep, however, was not square but cylindrical, with three projecting towers making the outside polygonal. Its curtain wall was set with towers at regular intervals, all round, offering no dead ground under cover of which the besiegers might batter or undermine the walls. The curtain wall, towers and all, has long since fallen and gone, but the keep, on its high ground, is preserved in excellent condition. You can climb the steps, explore the wall-galleries and garde-robes, and examine the maps on display showing the gradual extension of the river's sand-bank, spoiling the approach to the ports. You may notice that the habit of scratching graffiti on walls was irresistible at least as early as 1643. You can scale the steps to the roof and look out over the creek, the peculiarities of the river behind its sand-bank, and the sea.

If you return through the very pretty village, once town, of Orford, but follow the B1084 now, you will penetrate the tall, shadowy woodland of **Rendlesham Forest**, covering many more square miles of the Suffolk Sands. The soil has produced so little that it never has been a populous region. With the equally arid but much more extensive heathland in Suffolk and Norfolk north of Bury St Edmunds, it is the exception to the general rule of East Anglian fertility and remains largely uninhabited today.

The road arrives at and crosses the River Deben and you enter **Woodbridge**, which like all other Suffolk ports made a fortune from either wool or corn, its transport and export. In the days when road transport was unbelievably slow and therefore expensive, the sea was by far the quickest way of getting goods to market. Coastal shipping, despite the hazards, was intense until the coming of the railways. Woodbridge has plenty of sixteenth to eighteenth-century houses to show for its golden age.

At **Sutton Hoo**, on the other side of the river from Woodbridge, evidence was found in 1939 of earlier East Anglians, for a huge artificial mound was opened up and the remains of a ship found in it, the tomb or perhaps memorial of an East Anglian king of the early seventh century.

It is unfortunate but unavoidable that you must now use the main A12 road, since it is the best way of reaching the next objective, Colchester. **Ipswich** is basically an ancient town and retains some of its historic buildings, but it has not as much to offer as Colchester, so it may, if preferred, be bypassed by its ring-road system. The A12, by the gently hilly way between the river-vales of Orwell and Stour, will carry you to Colchester.

The principal concentration of interest in **Colchester** is in the castle, not only for itself but because of the marvellous museum it houses. It is at the eastern end of the town, so nearest to the direction from which you approach it.

Camulodunum was the town's name, and it was the capital of the tribe of Celtic Britons called *Trinobantes* before the Roman invasion and occupation of AD 43. It became the first deliberately created Roman colonial city, with a massive Temple of Claudius (the deified emperor). The inhabitants took shelter in this temple when Queen Boudicca of the *Iceni* came in AD 60 with avenging fury, slaughtered them all, and burnt the city. Fifty years later the Romans built walls all round it, with gates. The early English made Colchester (*Colonia-castra*) a thriving port again, and the Normans, when they found it expedient to defend it, used the existing massive base of the Temple of Claudius, still impervious to destruction after another 1,000 years, as a convenient foundation for their big thick castle walls. That is why Colchester Castle has the biggest keep in the country: it covers the temple area. Much material from the Roman city was evidently still about, because you can see its bricks and tiles in the Norman walls. The keep used to be much higher, but in 1683 it was bought for its building stone and partly demolished, like Canterbury. In 1931 it was roofed and equipped as a museum for the city's priceless store of relics from its long and turbulent past. Beneath it the Roman foundation vaults are accessible, and an enormous amount of Roman finds are on display.

Long stretches of the Roman city walls are visible, and beneath an inn called the *Hole in the Wall*, at the western end of the city, you can look through iron railings and see the remains of two archways of one of the gates.

Leaving Colchester by the same way back to the A12, the next excursion is to take the B1070 **East Bergholt** turning right to East Bergholt. This is an attractive group of typical East Anglian cottages with pink-washed plastered walls and thatched roofs, with an odd-looking church because its ring of bells is at ground level in a stumpy tower at its west end. John Constable, arguably the greatest of English landscape painters, was born in this village in 1776, lived in the area for some years, and threw himself into the problems of landscape painting, using the Stour vale as his source of subjects.

So many visitors are expected to the riverside now, to see Willy Lott's cottage and Flatford Mill, two of his subjects, that the lane from Flatford (an equally pretty village) terminates in an inescapable car park, with a fee demanded. Trees surrounding the vale obscure the view, so to pay homage to Constable this libation must be made.

You have to return to the A12 by the same route (more or less, for a one-way route has been devised) and once more circle Ipswich. This time, find the B1077 road to Diss and strike into the Suffolk countryside again, for the kind of landscape more familiar to Constable, perhaps, than his beloved Dedham Vale is today. There are few villages and little traffic, the scenery is serenely soothing and the whole effect ought to be therapeutic. Near a turning to Framsden you meet the A1120, on which you can turn right and then right again at Saxtead Green on the B1119 to Framlingham.

Framlingham   Framlingham Castle is at the top of the hill occupied by the little town, an eminence from which its garrison could watch over a broad extent of the River Alde valley. Although Henry II, exasperated with Earl Hugh of Norfolk's second rebellion against him, ordered the castle to be demolished, in 1178 the new earl, Hugh's son Roger, rebuilt it in a fashion similar to the king's own curtain wall around Orford, that is a high wall punctuated with obtruding square towers; but in this case there was no keep. What there is to be seen today is the complete circle of walls and towers, but none of the original domestic buildings within them. There is a later Poor House on the site of the Great Hall, but you have to look in its porch for Alan Sorrell's drawing to understand the layout. The artist has imagined the castle as it was when in use.

Saxmundham   The road back to Aldeburgh is the B1119 to the little town of Saxmundham, and a combination of A12, B1121, and A1094 over the heathland again and the golf course down to the salt-fresh Aldeburgh sea-front.

Norwich

Tourist Information Office
Augustine Stewart House, 14 Tombland, tel 20679

Population 120,100

Theatres
Maddermarket Theatre, St John's Alley
Theatre Royal, Theatre Street

Cinemas
ABC, Prince of Wales Road
Noverre, Assembly House, Theatre Street
Odeon, Anglia Square

Museums
Castle Museum and Art Gallery
Strangers Hall Museum, Charing Cross
Bridewell Museum, St Andrew's Lane

Places of Interest

Cathedral	Assembly House
Castle	Strangers' Hall
Fifteenth-century Guildhall	River Wensum

Unlike some others of England's old cathedral cities (Canterbury, Chichester, Winchester, for example), Norwich was not a city in Roman times. Traces of a town have been found at Caister St Edmund, a mile or two south, and this was *Venta Icenorum*, established as a result of Queen Boudicca's rebellion, as a means of keeping an eye on the Iceni. Norwich is therefore an East Anglian city, an important enough centre for William the Conqueror's Normans to build a stronghold on the hill above the River Wensum. This was replaced by a massive square stone keep between 1135 and 1150 when Hugh Bigod, Earl of Norfolk, asserted his powerful influence. The town prospered, and East Anglian fertility ensured that it became the biggest medieval city in England, after London.

The castle has been restored to something very like its original appearance, and now accommodates a large and comprehensive county museum, and a gallery for the work of the Norwich School of painting, which developed in the early nineteenth century. While Constable was working in his solitude, several painters in Norwich formed a society, notably Cotman, Crome, Ladbrooke, and Thirtle, and their theme, the same as Constable's, was the study of local landscape. Norwich at the period was unusual among provincial cities in developing a strong cultural element, and these painters, attracting others variable in talent, learned from each other and evolved sound principles in the technique of landscape painting. They were not unduly innovative, and few of them except Cotman ever achieved national or international recognition, but they produced a good deal of pleasing and sensitive work.

West of the Castle, across the street called Castle Meadow, you can go down to the Market Square (subject of one of Cotman's paintings, of 1807), presided over by the big church of St Peter Mancroft. At right angles to the church, replacing a row of medieval timbered buildings shown in Cotman's picture, is the awesome and imposing City Hall, relentlessly classical in style, and on the side opposite the church is the little flint-and-tile Guildhall of the fifteenth century. Behind the Guildhall a discreet lane slides down the hill by St John Maddermarket, to the Maddermarket Theatre, a new development tucked away among the old crooked houses. Continuing downhill towards the river the lanes emerge into the lateral St Benedict's Street, and a short way along on the left is a very old house called Strangers' Hall, which houses a museum.

Back along St Benedict's Street, close by St Andrew's Church a lane runs back up the hill, and on a corner is an old chemist's shop, now the Bridewell Museum of trades, crafts, and industries. Past St Andrew's Church the road leads into Prince's Street, which brings you to one of the cathedral gates.

The cathedral is a beautiful combination of Norman Romanesque and late Gothic. The nave, pure Norman, is superb, with arcade, triforium, and clerestory in regular exquisitely proportioned round-headed arches, and the fifteenth-century vaulted ceiling could not have blended more harmoniously if it had been made at the same time. The clean creamy-white stone gives an effect of marvellous light and purity. Outside, the proportions of this lovely building are further enhanced by its graceful fifteenth-century spire.

The River Wensum flows round three sides of the old city, and is full of moored boats. The river connects with the Yare and subsequently the other waterways of the Norfolk Broads, which means that holiday-boat-people have access to the city.

A typical example of a flourishing South-East English provincial capital, Norwich can offer more to interest visitors than I have had room to mention. Take a good street-map, explore it thoroughly, and you may discover many of the odd and fascinating corners.

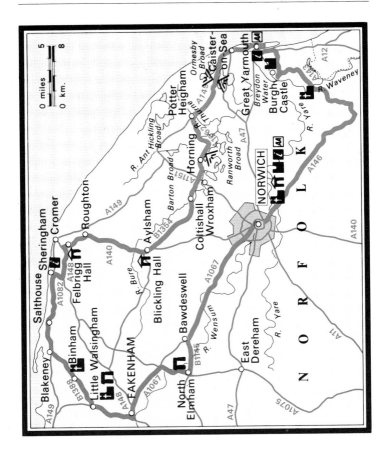

Norwich – North Elmham – Fakenham – Walsingham – Blakeney – Sheringham – Felbrigg Hall – Blickling Hall – Horning – Great Yarmouth – Burgh Castle – Norwich

Tour length 138 miles

As I have mentioned, although East Anglian distances tend to be greater than those in the south, motoring is made more pleasurable by the absence of much other traffic. Quite often, you can have the roads of North Norfolk to yourself. Except on the coast where there is a concentration of holiday resorts and consequently more traffic, there is no great density of population, either: villages are well-spaced, and small. Yet there are some important and fascinating archaeological sites, a centre for medieval pilgrimages, two great and magnificent country houses, and some of the best-known boating waters in the land.

From Norwich take the A1067 signposted Fakenham, which at once takes you away from the industrious Norwich perimeter and loses most of the traffic; then turn left at Bawdeswell on the B1145. Here is the high rolling wheatland of North Norfolk, fresh and airy, the light luminously bright; it is wonderful farmland, dark-soiled and prolific, yet it is not without tree cover. Much flint is used in the cottage walls, and some are thatched, but picturesque as this makes the villages, they are infrequent. Their churches are mostly small and plain, often with tall, slender towers.

At North Elmham turn left on the B1110. At the top of the hill, close by the fifteenth-century church, you will find the 1,000-year-old foundations of an Anglo-Saxon cathedral. The bishopric of North Elmham preceded that of Norwich: the diocesan cathedral, established in 910, was built in stone in the late tenth century. Its ground-plan is recognisable, in rough stone, flint, some Roman tiles and bricks, and much puddingstone, a natural agglomerate of ironstone. All the ingredients are held together by slabs of mortar. The ravages of time, normally responsible for delapidation, were in this case assisted by the desecration of the building by a blatantly irreligious fourteenth-century bishop of Norwich called Hugh Despenser, who adapted the ruins as a hunting lodge; some of the masonry is his work. Meticulously tidied and preserved by the Department of the Environment, this quiet and unfrequented spot is open most of the time and admission is free.

If you continue northwest on the B1110 you meet the A1067 again and can turn left on it, then left again on the A148 into Fakenham, an attractive and active little market town. Leave it on the A148 but turn off almost at once, right on **Little** the B1105 to Walsingham. There is a kind of **Walsingham** religious aura attached to Walsingham of a similar type, and for the same reason, as Lourdes: it has a shrine and is a place of pilgrimage. In fact it now has two shrines. Originally, a shrine was built by an eleventh-century lady of the manor after she had had a vision, and it became a popular focus of pilgrimages in the Middle Ages. An Augustinian priory was founded there in the thirteenth century, but little remains of the medieval structure which was dismantled at the Dissolution. The shrine suffered from zealous iconoclasm a little earlier, but was reconstructed by the Church of England in 1931. The Roman Catholics have their own, in the fourteenth-century Slipper Chapel a mile outside the village. A modern nunnery occupies the priory site, behind its ancient and battered gateway, and there are various fragments of masonry about showing the extent of medieval affluence resulting from the pilgrims' generosity. Most of the houses in the extremely picturesque village, however, are town houses of the sixteenth to eighteenth centuries, in timber and brick, which must testify to an alternative source of income: no doubt the land.

There are in fact two Walsinghams, and the one described in the above paragraph is Little. When you take the B1388 road to Blakeney you **Great** encounter Great Walsingham. The difference in **Walsingham** size, presumably meriting the distinctive adject-

Norwich Cathedral

ive, is not apparent. Hardly anyone seems to use the B1388, and there is plenty of time to look about, enjoy the balmy, wholesome air, distant glimpses of the sea, and a nearer view of Binham Priory, a 'cell' of the vastly important St Albans Abbey planted in 1091. Like Elstow at Bedford, the nave of its church had been used by the local parish before the Dissolution, and continued as the parish church when the priory ceased to exist.

Binham Priory

The North Norfolk coast has a very dense accumulation of sand, and the road that winds sinuously along the edge of the hills is often screened from the sea by a high dune. Blakeney has one of the tall-towered churches, set up on the hill behind it. All the villages are surrounded by a flood of holiday caravan encampments. Cley-next-the-Sea (where a restaurant on a hair-raisingly sharp corner is called the Change Down) and Salthouse have a fresh-fish flavour, and Sheringham is a cheerful seaside holiday town. All of these places, well patronised during the summer season, are full of inns and restaurants advertising all imaginable varieties of seafood.

Blakeney

Cley-next-the-Sea

Sheringham

Turn right out of Sheringham on the A1082, then quickly left on the A148. You are still on the sand-dune belt, as you can see by the thick pine-woods about you. You are on the road to Cromer, but turn off right on the B1436 and into Felbrigg Hall's long drive, lined with an avenue of oaks which could be two hundred years old, to see a grand Jacobean mansion with tall stone-mullioned windows, its high frontage surmounted by a stone frieze spelling out GLORIA DEO IN EXCELSIS, and adjoined by an eighteenth-century stable and service block. Its surrounding park and woodland are celebrated and very extensive.

Felbrigg Hall

Carry on along the B1536 until you meet the A140 and emerge from the sand-and-forest belt. This is Roughton, where the *New Inn*, on the main road, can well supply your wants.

Roughton

The A140 is smooth and fast, and soon you are at the turning right to Ingworth and Blickling, signs to which can be followed. The entrance to Blickling Hall is on the B1354 road to Aylsham.

Blickling Hall

Blickling is a grander and more sumptuous version of Felbrigg. Its splendid, spectacular front with onion-spired towers and a central clock-tower, extends two long service wings on either side of a green-lawned courtyard, flanked by impeccably trimmed yew hedges. Every window in the sides and rear of the house has a prospect of the vast and immaculately land-scaped garden and parkland, including the statu-tory lake fringed with graceful trees. The house is full of fine pictures and furniture, much of it collected from the countries visited by the 2nd Earl of Buckinghamshire in the eighteenth century in the course of his duties as an ambassador. The full visitors' tour includes two floors, with such glories as the dining-room, where the long table is set for sixteen, with late seventeenth-century chairs, glass, and silver-plate but engagingly fresh flowers. There are tapestries, moulded plaster ceilings, and a long gallery turned into a library, with thousands of books whose titles seem to indicate that many are unread and probably unreadable, but serve their purpose as decoration.

Blickling, the home of the Hobart family, was completed by the second baronet, Sir John. The estate was willed in 1940 to the National Trust, who tend it and have occupied the entire east service wing with their offices and shop.

A family in long possession of a great and beautiful house, built by an ancestor, can fill it with objects collected and accumulated by each generation, with differing taste and opportunity, but the result is uniquely homogeneous, since all things diminish when placed in their allotted corner of the house itself, and those which are not of eternal beauty diminish further. 'Truth in all things,' Constable wrote, 'only will last, and can only have just claims on posterity.' Whether or not one approves of one family having so much and keeping it for so long through inheritance, it is impossible to imagine how such houses, multiplied throughout the country and mostly now available for all to see and appreciate, could have come to exist without such wealth-based continuity.

From the gates of Blickling Hall the B1354 goes

Aylsham to Aylsham, and thence into the region known as the Norfolk Broads. These comprise a network of rivers and lakes which since the 1939–1945 war have become increasingly popular for boating holidays. The lakes, called Broads, were formed when medieval Norfolk people dug beside the rivers for peat, which could be burnt as fuel. The extensive diggings filled with water, in which reeds grew abundantly, and these were cut, dried, and used for thatching. Fish and eels abounded, as did waterfowl, and until the twentieth century no one thought of the Broads except as an area which could be profitably exploited for its natural produce.

The twentieth-century holiday mania brought a vast influx of temporary boatmen, seriously reduced the natural produce, and fouled the water. Despite this the Broads retain their fascination for any who have sailed in them and fathomed their mysteries. The B1354, although it serves the northern waters, actually touches them only rarely. It crosses the Bure at *Coltishall* Coltishall, where it is quite narrow, misses the yachting headquarters at Wroxham, but then *Horning* joins the A1062 and runs close by Horning, which is accessible by a side-road. You come to the river by the *Swan Hotel*, and as you pass by the houses you can see that, old or new, they all display some connection with boats or fishing: those actually on the river-bank have their own boat-houses and landing-stages. By the *New Inn* there is a way to the river where you can see up and down Horning Reach on the Bure, smell that exciting old river-smell, hear the lapping of the water on the banks and against the boat-hulls, watch the coots bobbing their white heads as they try hazardously to cross the water, and the occasional boat puttering past, or gliding silently, the top triangle of sail catching a breath of the light breeze over the encircling willows. The Broads have a magic of their own: early morning, or late evening, preferably out of season, is the best time to discover it.

The road crosses the Ant at Ludham and the *Potter* Thurne at Potter Heigham, another boat-hirers' *Heigham* metropolis, but you have still not set eyes on a Broad, only the rivers. But take the A149 from

Potter Heigham: it lets you drive along a causeway between Ormesby and Rollesby Broads, and you can see then how you are obliged to stop and stare. Actually, these two are not navigable by the hired boats, but as you will see, plenty of sailing is done on both of them, and their shining, glittering, tree-fringed expanse, so inviting to resident and visiting water-birds, equally invites you to stay a while and admire it.

Caister-on-Sea   You reach the coast again near Caister-on-Sea, where there was another small Roman town with strong walls. The road joins the extraordinary sea-front promenade of Great Yarmouth, dis-tinguished by a staggering succession of amuse-ments and excitements of all imaginable descrip-tions. Great Yarmouth used to be an important fishing port, and many were the pitched battles between its seamen and those of the Cinque Ports over some matter of marketing or fishing rights. Little is left of those sterner days, but if you drive on past the gaudy manifestations of our pleasure-seeking age, then turn right, you will come to the docks, which are on the mouth of the combined rivers Bure, Yare, and Waveney, whose basins constitute the entire Broads system. On the right of South Quay, the road that runs alongside the river, is a merchant's house of the sixteenth century, which is a museum, open most of the time for most of the day. It has a later frontage, but it is a survivor of those hardier times. Trading ships still moor and load at the quayside, too, to show that the town is not yet entirely effete. You cross the bridge across the river on the A143, and at the roundabout where the A12 begins, a lane to the right, signposted Burgh Castle, leads into caravan-infested country on the rising ground overlooking Breydon Water, a huge basin fed by the rivers Yare and Waveney.

Burgh   At the end of Burgh village, a lane goes to its tiny parish church, which has a cylindrical tower. There is a car park below the churchyard, and a footpath beside it. A long walk, beside a field and across it at the end, brings you to the substantial walls of Burgh Castle. This was *Gariannonum*, a Roman fort of the Saxon Shore, defending the vulnerable interior from attack by German sea-pirates, sailing up the wide rivers; it

was garrisoned until the early fifth century. A
monastery was built within its stout walls in the
seventh century, and a Norman earth-and-wood
castle in the eleventh, but unlike Pevensey and
Portchester, this was not replaced in stone.
Oblong in shape, with solid semi-circular bastions attached, on the top of which the powerful
siege-catapults called *ballistae* could be em-
placed, the west wall overlooking the water has
gone, leaving the other three standing: they are
still up to a few feet of their original height.

It has been a long tour: there is still St Olave's
Priory, close by the bridge by which the A143
crosses the Waveney, but it is yet a long drive
back to Norwich, by this A143 and the A146.
They are both good, fast roads, and like most in
Norfolk uncrowded.

Index